The Labrador Saga

James Milton Hanna

The Labrador Saga
James Milton Hanna
Copyright 2005

ISBN 1-930052-31-6
Library of Congress Number 2005908435

Library of Congress Cataloging in Publication Data.
James Milton Hanna
The Labrador Saga
Experiences of a member of the USAF stationed at Goose Bay, Labrador, Canada in the early 1950s
Rescue, survival, native lore, outdoor living and work as a Military Scout.

Printed in the United States of America by
Quill Publications—Columbus, GA

Other Books by Author

Cornbread and Beans for Breakfast
A Possum in Every Pot
Beyond Yonder Ridge
A Man Called Shiloh
Southern Tales
Milton's Guide to Self Publishing
Tales from Delaware Bay
More Tales from Delaware Bay
Once Upon a Time in the South
Meandering Around Delaware Bay

Cherokee Books • 231 Meadow Ridge Pkwy
Dover, DE 19904

Acknowledgments/Dedication

To all servicemen who have served at APO 677, Goose Bay, Labrador.

To the 54th Air Sea Rescue Squadron whose motto is "That Others May Live."

To those brave Airmen who lost their lives flying in and out of Goose Bay.

To Corporal Kenneth Jones for his dedication in helping operate The Survival School at Goose.

Rev. Paul Judson MacKinney, his wife Rena, and son, Rev. Danny MacKinney. May their dedication to God not be forgotten.

To the native people who I grew to appreciate.

To Donna Chappell for editing this book.

Table of Contents

Introduction

When we grow older, we often look back at the experiences of our youth. Sometimes we think of those times as our finest times in life. Milton thinks of his Air Force assignment to Goose Bay, Labrador as the most meaningful time in his life.

This book is a true story of the unique experiences of a boy from Alabama, who entered the Air Force when he was barely seventeen. He was born and lived in North Alabama his entire life until the events depicted in these pages.

Perhaps his experiences paralleled that of many other young men who entered the service during that time. Most joined one branch of the armed forces or another for the experience, patriotism, or to escape the draft. Maybe they figured it better to choose the branch of service one wanted to serve, rather than wait to be drafted. Milton volunteered to serve his country in the Air Force.

Milton was a high school dropout who loved the outdoors and spent many years pursuing various aspects of God's creation. Perhaps he was listening to a different drumbeat than many of his peers. Before he entered the service he had read everything he could find in the local high school libraries pertaining to the arctic.

Milton's first military assignment outside the United States was Goose Bay, Labrador. Mentally, he was prepared for that assignment and eagerly looking forward to a land of tall Black Spruce trees, bubbling brooks, white water rivers and numerous lakes of various sizes filled with crystal clear waters.

The icy mountains and deep forests of Labrador beckoned Milton. The deep snow, ice-covered streams, lakes and the apparition of the Northern Lights flashed across the skies completely mesmerized him. From the first day at that assignment he felt a sense of belonging and fulfillment of destiny like he had finally come home.

The three years spent at Goose Bay were action packed because of the nature of Milton's job. The assignment was normally for one year, but he extended six months at a time until he had spent three years there. He matured more in those three years (age 17-20) than any time in his life. Some of the incidents he was involved in were a matter of life and death.

Several incidents Milton could have handled differently. His was a learning experience. Many incidents were omitted from this book for personal reasons. Perhaps they are still too painful to discuss.

Some will perhaps relate to some of the stories

in this book. Milton's assignment to Goose Bay, Labrador wasn't a routine assignment. May you read this book and gain an appreciation of what it was like to have been a member of the armed forces and assigned to an isolated base in an unusual capacity.

James Milton Hanna
2005

−1−

The Remote Duty Assignment

The military assignment orders read: APO 677, Goose Bay, Labrador. "Where in the world is Labrador?" Milton wondered as he re-read his orders and noticed the date to report to Camp Kilmer, New Jersey for a flight to his new assignment. He was to be reassigned to an isolated duty station for one year. "One year isn't bad," Milton thought. "Some overseas assignments are for three years."

Milton was seventeen and had already completed basic training at Lackland AFB, Texas, the Military Police Academy at Camp Gordon, Georgia and now he was finishing a four month assignment to a Military Police Squadron at Westover AFB, Mass.

Basic training had been a snap. He had been in such good physical condition from years of outdoor living that he hadn't minded the marching, long hikes with full field packs, or other activities associated with basic training. His thirteen week training program passed fast. He made several new friends and as usual, the situation with military men, parted company when graduating from basic training. He and his companions were sent to various bases in the US for specialized training in their assigned career fields.

Milton had enjoyed the one weekend pass received at the end of the tenth week of basic training. He spent an entire Saturday in San Antonio walking from one point of interest to another, especially the Alamo. Finally, with a friend, appropriately nicknamed Tex, because he was from Comanche, Texas, located riding stables at Fort Sam Houston and rented horses for a part of the day.

The horses had been ridden by so many people that they seemed to evaluate each rider and then decide how to behave. Late in the afternoon the horses sensed that it was oat-eating time and headed in a beeline for the stables. There was nothing Milton or Tex could do to prevent the horses from returning to the stables. Each horse managed to get the bit between its teeth so that the rider couldn't control them and then to show contempt, they brushed against trees in an effort to cause pain and suffering to the riders. Only when they were allowed to head toward the stables did they behave. Riding the horses had been fun anyway.

Later in the evening, Tex and Milton were following a path on the shore of the San Antonio River, a small dirty stream filled with whiskey and beer bottles, and tires in most areas, and according to the newspapers on several occasions, bodies of people who had been murdered. The San Antonio River wouldn't have been considered even a small creek where Milton had lived in Alabama. During their walk, they noticed three men from their squadron seated at a table located on a patio outside a bar on the bank of the river drinking beer. With them were three attractive, but not to young Mexican ladies.

The men invited them to stop and have a drink. The table was filled with several already emptied bottles. The men appeared already intoxicated. Milton and his friend declined the invitation. The men said that the three girls had friends who would date them if they wanted. Again, they declined. Three weeks later these men had to go on sick call because of having contracted a social disease they apparently picked up from their dates. Milton and Tex got a good laugh because the three men had to report to sick call for penicillin shots for several days.

Tex and Milton corresponded with each other for a year, and by then the Korean War had started. Tex never returned to his beloved Camache, Texas. Tex, and like many other young men during that period, suffered the greatest sacrifice. He was killed in action in Korea, as well as several of Milton's friends.

Milton had volunteered to be a Military Policeman. At that time the Military Police was an elite force consisting of all volunteers. Anyone desiring to or who becoming despondent as a policeman could request another assignment. Milton liked the option of being able to select his career field. He turned down an assignment to become a supply man, radio operator or cook. He thought being a policeman would be more exciting. And sometimes it proved to be too exciting.

On June 27, 1949, Milton rode a train to Camp Gordon, which is located on the outskirts of Augusta, Georgia. The weather was scorching – like all summers in Georgia – but Texas had been hot too. Milton was assigned to Company D, of the Military Police Academy. The barracks were old World War II, open bay barracks that were kept surprisingly cool by the huge fans in the ceilings.

The training was tough and very educational. Milton probably matured more from the Academy than from any previous experience. Again, he developed friendships with several other trainees, and whenever there was spare time, Milton and his friends spent happy hours roaming the woodland on the huge Army Reservation. They developed skills in throwing knifes and hatchets. Milton sighted his first Black Squirrels and was able to scare several with his throwing knives. He purposely missed because he had no way to cook a squirrel and it was wrong to kill just for fun. They played like a bunch of young Indians.

Part of the training consisted of six weeks of combat Judo. Milton and his friends became somewhat expert in the art of learning how to disable and kill with their bare hands. Also, many hours were spent on the Firing Range learning to master various types of weapons and throwing grenades. Probably the most dangerous part of the Academy was learning to direct traffic in downtown Augusta. The drivers showed little respect for the Military Police Trainees who were doing their best at the intersections to keep traffic flowing smoothly. Milton had to jump out of the way once to keep from being run over. Somehow, he survived and was able to graduate with a respectful grade. Not bad for a high school drop out.

Milton was kept at Camp Gordon an extra month for training with the Military Police Town Patrol Unit. He really felt like a policeman when patrolling downtown. The "strip"– a road with many bars, pawn shops and dance halls, most being off limits to military personnel – was dangerous to patrol.

Many incidents occurred during those patrols. When Milton and the Sergeant, to whom he was assigned for training, entered one of the off-limit bars to check for Military Personnel, the conversation and music would stop and everyone would stare at them. When they walked out the door, conversation and music would start again. It gave Milton a weird feeling to enter any of those establishments. The military police were treated like an enemy. Perhaps they were indeed enemies to the soldiers who were breaking military law by being in the off-limit areas.

One night, Milton was scared half to death when several of the people in one of the bars they checked yelled "Lets get these M.P.s," and stood up from their tables and advanced toward Milton and the Sergeant. Milton didn't know what to do. He was scared. He could imagine being hit over the head with a beer bottle. He reached for his .45 and was hesitant in drawing it from his holster. The sergeant didn't hesitate. He drew his pistol and the men coming toward them suddenly decided to sit down at the table they had just gotten up from.

The Sergeant and Milton backed out the door of the bar and leaped into their patrol jeep and made a fast getaway. Milton later discovered that the Sergeant had been a Combat Military Policeman during all of WW II. Those people in the bar didn't know how lucky they were, because if they hadn't backed down, the Sergeant wouldn't have hesitated to have shot them. His name was Sergeant Armstrong. Milton remembered that he walked with a limp from being wounded by a sniper in France. Common sense dictated that there were too many soldiers in that off-limits area for the two M.P.s to attempt arresting them. From the nearest phone the M.P. Officer was notified and soon several loads of Military Policemen raided that bar and over a dozen soldiers were in deep trouble.

All of the students in the Academy were much older. Personnel from all branches of the military attended the prestigious Military Police Academy at Fort Gordon located near Augusta, Georgia. Milton felt honored to have been afforded the opportunity to attend the academy.

Oct 15, 1949 Milton received orders to report to Westover AFB, located near Springfield, Mass. He was to be a member of the 1600th Military Police Squadron. Milton was given a ride to Augusta's Train Depot. The train ride was uneventful until he reached Grand Central Station in New York City and had to change stations to catch a train to Springfield, Mass. He had never been to a city as huge as New York City. He couldn't help but gawk at the tall buildings. To him the city was large and dirty, and the people were something else. Everyone was in a hurry and very unfriendly. He had nodded to several people and they had ignored him.

Milton had arrived at Grand Central Station with only twenty-one cents in his pocket. He had to catch a bus to another station. The bus fare was twenty cents. Milton never forgot that short bus ride. He was carrying a large duffel bag and an old metal suit case containing all of his worldly goods. It was October, but a hot day and he was wearing a wool dress uniform. He was perspiring from every pore by the time he arrived at the train station. Once on the train he was able to purchase lunch with a meal ticket issued to him with his train ticket. The military personnel were given meal tickets when traveling by train. The train was cool and he slept the rest of the way to the new assignment.

Assignment to the Military Police Squadron caused Milton to feel like a real policeman and he would finally be able to work in the job that he had been trained. While assigned to Westover, Milton worked on patrol, gate guard, special guard and honor guards.

On the night shift, at 1130, Milton was assigned to guard duty at the Base morgue. That job was his first assignment working alone. It was a cold, foggy night, with a light misty rain falling when Milton was posted at the building that served as a morgue. The building was situated a few hundred feet from the nearest building, and located on top of a small hill in a grove of oak trees.

The guard that Milton relieved was standing outside in the rain waiting to be relieved. Milton wondered why the guard was standing outside in the rain instead of inside where it was warm and dry. The Sergeant in charge took Milton inside the morgue and informed him that it was his station for the night. "I'll see you at seven in the morning," the Sergeant informed Milton.

The morgue was a four-room house. In the front room were three coffins. Each was covered with an American flag. One of the flags had become wrinkled so Milton started to straighten it and it fell off to one side of the coffin. The coffin had a glass viewing section and there in front of Milton was an officer dressed in full uniform with medals. Milton had never seen a dead person before and was startled. He quickly repositioned the flag with trembling hands.

Milton decided to explore the other rooms of the morgue. What was hidden behind the closed doors was a mystery. He opened the door and switched the lights on. The adjoining room contained a refrigerated unit built into the wall. There were eight small compartments. Milton was curious and opened a small door and inside was a sliding tray containing a body. He quickly slammed the door. He was almost trembling with fright by that time.

The remaining rooms were filled with six occupied coffins. Milton moved his chair next to the front door and attempted to relax. Occasionally, he would start to doze and at that time the compressor for the refrigerated unit would start with a loud noise, scaring Milton all over again. He was a nervous wreck in a short time.

In the wee hours of the morning, Milton heard a noise. He looked up and saw a hand reaching up and scratching on the outside of the window across the room from him. Milton was so scared that he immediately drew his .45 caliber pistol, injected a bullet into the chamber, and almost pulled the trigger when his Sergeant yelled "Don't shoot." Milton thought that he was really in trouble. The sergeant came in, somewhat shaken, and told Milton that he had stopped to see how he was doing and had brought him coffee.

The sergeant apologized for trying to scare Milton like he did. He said that he shouldn't have done that. Milton agreed. He told the Sergeant that he had done a good job scaring him. He was still shaking.

After a few nights as honor guard at the morgue, Milton was able to sleep. He locked the front door so that if anyone came, they would have to knock on the door to get in and that would awaken him. The Sergeant in charge of his shift said that it was okay for persons stationed at the morgue to nap. It was a good thing that he was able to nap during that assignment because most days when he was off duty he had to be on an honor guard at funerals for returning WW II dead.

Milton was finally assigned to other guard duties, including the main gate. On the way to post guards, Milton and other men who were to be assigned to different posts for the night dropped a man off at the morgue. The morgue was a quarter of a mile from the main road. After the relief had driven to one of the base's entrance gates and was on the way back, the guard they had posted at the morgue was already back to the main road awaiting them.

When the Sergeant stopped the vehicle to inquire why the man had left his post, the man said,

"You can lock me up or do anything you want with me, but I will not stay in that morgue with all of them dead bodies." Everyone got a laugh from that incident. The kid was assigned to another post. He was from Georgia and possessed a phobia of being near dead people.

One evening when Milton was working the main gate to the base, a car left the main highway and drove toward the gate. As customary, all cars had to stop and the occupants identified. Milton stepped into the middle of the road and held his hand up palm out indicating for the driver to stop and identify himself. To Milton chagrin, the car never slowed and Milton had to leap from its path or else be run over. He drew his pistol and started to fire a round after the fleeing car, but decided that might not be a wise choice.

A car, following the car that had failed to stop, was identified as being driven by a Major assigned to the Base. He told Milton that he would pursue the car and attempt to stop it. Milton immediately phoned Military Police Headquarters and the chase was on. Finally, the fleeing car was stopped.

The driver had been involved in an accident at a traffic circle outside the Base and had suffered a concussion and apparently was driving in a daze, not knowing where he was going. His car had upset and was righted by other motorists. Milton was glad that he hadn't shot at the fleeing car. The poor man had enough problems without being shot to further complicate matters.

The few months spent at Westover were mostly uneventful and passed slowly. Milton and a good friend decided to start riding horses that could be rented at the Base stables. The riding was fun, and the horse proved better behaved than the one he had ridden in Texas. Finally, one day they decided to stop horse back riding because of an incident that almost got them into trouble.

It happened this way; one rainy day when everything was wet, they were riding and decided to explore more of the Base. They departed from the regular bridal trail and ventured into a Base housing area. There were beautiful and large homes there. They rode at a gallop through some of the yards. Soon someone reported them to the Police and the chase was on. They kept out of sight of the pursuing vehicles and hid in the woods near the perimeter road. There were several horses checked out that day, so they were able to return their faithful steeds to the stable without incident. They decided to give up riding horses for a time until things cooled off somewhat.

The Commanding General of the Base didn't take lightly people riding through his lawn and leaving deep tracks. All kinds of new directives were written for the Base Riding Stables governing rider's conduct and limiting where horses could be ridden on Base. Milton and his friend, Howard Tabor, felt guilty about the incident, but not guilty enough to confess to the incident that caused so much grief to the riding stables. They felt that Generals and Colonels wouldn't be too understanding of the actions of two privates.

Milton was assigned mail guard duty once each week. He worked the 12-8 shift most of the time. The guard duty at the Transient Mail Building was a disliked post. The building was large and one wall was divided into small partitions for mail bags. Each partition was labeled with the name of an overseas Base where mail was delivered. Milton had never before heard most of the names.

There were three Bases in Newfoundland, two in Greenland, one in Goose Bay, Labrador, Iceland, Scotland, and Bases in England and continental Europe. These names had little meaning to Milton as he paced back and forth throughout the building guarding the mail.

The Transient Mail Building was a cold post in the winter. There was no heat in the building except for a small office and the mail guard was never invited there. The NCOIC of that division didn't like Military Policemen for some reason. Perhaps, he had experienced a traffic ticket or had been written up for some other infraction of the law and now his anger was directed toward the mail guards.

Milton would observe people entering the office and drinking piping hot coffee while he paced back and forth freezing to death. His shift supervisor would bring him a cup of coffee at least once each shift. That wasn't sufficient. Milton thought that entering the office and warming up occasionally would be nice. Neither he nor any other guards that he knew were ever invited into that office for coffee or to enjoy the heat.

The Air Force was different in those days. Milton remembered his first payday at Westover. Everyone was paid in cash once per month in the day room. Milton's pay was seventy dollars a month. The day room was a recreation room with pool tables and other games.

The first time he was paid at Westover AFB, Milton noticed that everyone remained in the building after they were paid.Immediately after the last man had signed for and received his pay, the Squadron Commander, First Sergeant and several other individuals started throwing dice and dealing cards.

Soon the day room looked like a Reno casino. Almost everyone was gambling. Milton didn't gamble because he thought it wrong, and he received so little money that he could ill afford to lose any. His mother was a widow and he sent any spare money to her to help with his younger sister's education. He often observed some of the men losing their entire pay and having to borrow money to see them through the month. Some of the men loaned money at a return of two to one. i.e. borrow five and repay ten.

December 5, 1949 was an eventful day for

Milton. He received orders to ship out on the last day of January for Goose Bay, Labrador, located several hundred miles North of Boston, Massachusetts, in Northeast Canada, for a one year assignment. It was an interesting fact that over half of the Police Squadron received shipping orders at that same time. His new friends were shipped to Newfoundland, Goose Bay, Labrador, Greenland, Iceland and Korea. Several failed to survive the Korean War that started June 26, 1950.

Those orders were the start of an exciting three years. Milton immediately went to the base library and read all the material he could locate about Labrador. He discovered that Goose Bay was located about two hundred miles inland from the Atlantic Ocean and was kept cold by the Labrador current flowing South from Baffin Island and Greenland.

That part of Labrador was considered sub-Arctic and often received several feet of snow each winter with temperatures dropping to forty degrees below zero. The people were mostly hunters, trappers and fishermen. Most of the people barely subsisted in that harsh climate. Labrador was a part of Newfoundland and was to soon be joined with Newfoundland as a providence to Canada. Milton thought from reading about Labrador that everything sounded just like the Arctic he had read so much about while living in Alabama.

−2−

Goose Bay AFB, Labrador

February 2, 1950 was when Milton and several other replacements arrived at Goose Bay, Labrador aboard a C-54. The flight from Camp Kilmer, New Jersey had been an interesting flight.

Milton spent the entire flight, and this was his first flight, looking out the small windows of the plane. The country they flew over was snow covered. He recognized the Gulf of Saint Lawrence by its width. The entire gulf was ice covered and rough sections were visible from where ice-breakers had made a futile effort to keep the ship channel open.

The North shore of the gulf was carpeted with conifer, most likely spruce, fir, and juniper trees. Occasionally, white birch trees could be seen along streams, most of which were frozen except for sections of rapids. Flying at eight thousand feet allowed for a view equal to the most beautiful of scenic post cards.

The newness of flight and viewing such beauty was an experience that Milton will always remember. The land was void of human habitation for mile after mile. It was only after the plane was approaching Goose Bay to land that Milton observed a small cluster of buildings located on a river a few miles from the base.

There was a break in the trees indicating a road leading from the village to the Base. (Later he discovered that the small cluster of shacks was the Happy Valley settlement) While the plane was circling the Base for a landing, Milton observed a huge body of ice covered water and blue-white mountains in the distance. The mountains were mostly barren and snow covered. The Mealy Mountains were located on the southern shore of Lake Melville.

The aircraft taxied to the Base Terminal where Milton and the other replacements were directed down the ramp and into the Flight Terminal. All of the new arrivals were shivering from the cold by the time they walked the two hundred feet to the building. The heat felt good. The temperature was ten degrees above zero.

Neither, Milton nor the other men wore Arctic Clothing. They were wearing their issue overcoats and regular issue shoes. Everyone they saw was dressed in parkas with fur around the hoods, large mittens, and heavy trousers and shoe pack boots. Milton felt out of place dressed like he was. He and the other new arrivals stood out like a sore thumb. Their very appearance screamed "Newcomer."

The new arrivals were directed to a briefing room where they were placed into the charge of a member of the organization where they were to be assigned. The men were briefed about the dangers of frostbite and given instructions on how to avoid frostbite when exposed to the merciless cold and wind.

Milton was told that the Base was a joint Canadian-American base. There were four hundred men assigned to Goose and there were about the same number of Indians, Newfoundlanders, and Canadians living in Happy Valley. Goose Bay was a refueling stopover for planes flying to Greenland, Iceland and the United Kingdom.

Goose also functioned as a refueling stop for planes re-supplying bases further north. A large sign- "GOOSE BAY, THE GATEWAY TO THE ARCTIC" was posted over the door to the Base Flight Operations Building.

There were a few Newfoundland girls employed as secretaries in some of the offices and workers in the Base Exchange, Cafeteria, Non-Commissioned Officers Club and in the Officer's Club. There were about twenty men for each female assigned to the Base. And some of the women were married. The Sergeant giving the briefing cautioned the men to have nothing to do with the few native girls from the Happy Valley Settlement.

After the briefing, Milton was taken to the Base Supply Building and issued the required winter clothing. After dressing warmly in his new clothing, Milton felt like Jack London up in the Yukon. The person assigned to him gave a guided tour of the few buildings cluster together. His barracks was next to the Dining Hall. The Base Exchange and Police Headquarters were across the street from the barracks. He didn't have far to walk to work or to the Dining Hall. He was told to report to work for another briefing the next morning at eight o'clock.

While being shown around, Milton couldn't believe that snow could be so deep. The single-story buildings had snow drifted against them so that a person, that is if he wanted to, could walk to the roof. The Spruce trees were loaded with snow and the roads were packed snow. Nowhere was there a single bit of exposed dirt or grass. Everything was white, with a contrasting gray or green buildings and trees.

The Spruce trees looked like Christmas trees with snow hanging from their limbs. A sign was nailed to a Spruce tree with an arrow pointed down a snow- covered road. The sign read "SKI SLOPE". Milton had read so many books about the Arctic and North Country that he felt qualified to ski. That would be an experience to write home about. After all, Alabama never had snow such as was found at Goose Bay. (He remembered that in 1940 it had snowed six inches that winter in north Alabama.)

A sign labeled "Special Services" pointed to a building across the street from the Base Exchange. Milton entered and checked out a pair of skis. (He couldn't complete processing into the Base until the next day, so why not have fun skiing.) Skiing looked so easy from the pictures and movies that he had seen.

The walk to the Ski Slope was about a mile on snow packed roads. The Skiing Area was a long, steep hill. From the vantage- point on top of the Ski Slope, Milton could see trees extending to a large river (it was frozen too) and then on the far side of the river were more trees and small mountains as far as he could see. It was nothing but wilderness, just the type of land where Milton had dreamed of someday living. It reminded him of all the stories he had read of the North Country.

Milton laced on the ski shoes and attached the borrowed skis. He found that walking on skis wasn't as easy as it had appeared. Somehow he stumbled to the edge of the slope, and taking a deep breath, dug the ski poles into the snow and catapulted down the slope. He must have remained upright for the first ten feet. After that he tumbled all the way down the slope to the bottom. The slope was steep, much too steep for a novice.

When he finally skidded to a halt in the deep snow at the foot of the slope, he lay in the snow afraid to move for a moment. His body felt like every bone was broken. Lucky for him, there were no broken bones, only several pulled muscles and a light spring of one ankle. Somehow, he removed the one remaining ski — one ski had come loose half way down the slope — and made his way slowly and painfully back up the slope to where he had started.

He was the only one at the ski area so he felt better when he realized that no one was there to observe his disgraceful tumble all the way down the slope. He painfully limped back to the Special Services Building and returned the skis.

For the remaining three years at Goose Bay, he never checked out another pair of skis or attempted to ski. He returned to the barracks, took a hot shower and immediately went to sleep.

Early the next morning Milton was awake at 6:30. It was still dark. After shaving and dressing warmly, he walked across the street to the Mess Hall for breakfast. Breakfast consisted of toast, powdered milk, powdered orange juice, powered eggs, and rancid bacon. He discovered that food supplies came in by ship from late June through August. Supplies were getting low this late in the season.

Before eight, Milton was at the Police Station to meet the officer In Charge and the NCO on whose shift he would be working. The Officer's name was Lt. McGowan. He stood six foot six and was a World War II veteran. He had won his commission on the battle- field in Europe. There were eighteen men assigned to the Police Squadron. Work hours were 12 on and 36 hours off.

Milton was assigned to the night shift under a Sgt Fodor. He was issued a .45 caliber pistol, two clips of ammunition and a club. He spent two hours being briefed about his job and responsibilities. He was given a fast tour of the American and Canadian side of the Base by jeep. Snow was piled six to eight feet alongside the road. He was told to report for duty before six that afternoon. He was to start on the night shift.

Milton eagerly reported for duty and was told that he would be a patrolman the first six hours and an Aircraft Hanger Guard the remaining six hours of each shift. Milton had a small problem: He had never driven a vehicle before. He was embarrassed to inform Sgt Fodor that he couldn't drive. Sgt Fodor looked like he couldn't believe a seventeen-year old couldn't drive. He asked Milton if he had been raise in the hills of Alabama or Georgia where there were no automobiles. "Well, yes, I'm from Alabama." He answered.

The Sergeant just shook his head in disbelief and told Milton they were going for a ride. They drove to the Motor Pool where the other patrol jeep was located. Sgt. Fodor gave Milton a ten-minute driving lesson and told him that he would check the "G" Area, located on the far side of the Base, once each hour. The Sergeant drove away leaving Milton with the patrol jeep. Before he departed, he handed Milton a shovel. Milton asked what the shovel was for. Sgt. Fodor told him that he would soon find out.

Milton attempted to shift into first gear and many gears ground together. Finally, he was able to depress the clutch properly and shift into second gear and drove to "G" Area for his hourly check. He soon discovered what the reason for the shovel. He must have gotten stuck six times on the way to "G" Area.

He had to shovel the jeep out of several snow banks when the jeep skidded. Some parts of the road were rutted fifteen inches deep. Overall, Milton was proud of himself for being able to master driving the jeep so quickly. The other Policemen found it amusing that he didn't know how to drive. He took a lot of ribbing because of not knowing how to drive. Overall everyone was very friendly.

Soon he was able to shift all the gears without grinding a single gear. Learning to drive on snow-packed roads was very beneficial to Milton in later years. He never found any of the "Ice Snakes" that Sergeant Fodor had warned him about. (It seemed that all newcomers were warned about Ice Snakes which of course didn't exist)

While patrolling with the jeep, Milton almost ran into a dog team on the road to the Canadian side of the Base. Milton went to work in the dark and when relieved each morning it was still dark. He was driving along and saw something in his headlights and to evade that obstacle drove into a snow bank. The obstacle was a dog team approaching.

As he sat behind the wheel, the dogs passed next to his jeep. There were five huge, wolf-like dogs pulling a flat sled almost silently past where the jeep came to rest in the snow bank. A small fur-clad figure sat on a large box tied on the front of the sled. Milton recognized him to be an Eskimo. He gave Milton a big smile as the dogs panted past the jeep.

Milton was thrilled seeing his first dog team. He had seen pictures of dog teams before, but this was different. If he had dared, he could have reached out and touched the dogs as they padded past with tails curled over their backs. The dogs looked too fierce and wolf-like to touch. Milton was excited to see a real dog team after reading about that type of transportation for years. It took twenty minutes of shoveling to free the jeep from the snow bank.

Milton's first week of Patrol and Guard Duty went well. He learned the location of different buildings on the Base, and met the other men who were assigned to his Squadron. His horse-riding friend from Westover Air Force Base arrived at Goose Bay soon after Milton. Milton and Howard Tabor were friends and had done many things together. He was a former Army man who had joined the Air Force when his time in the Army was completed. He was an exceptional and very talented man. He had turned down an appointment to West Point. He was a few years older that Milton, but they got along very well together.

One thing about the other men in his Squadron that he didn't like was that everyone had a calendar and marked off each day in anticipation of finishing their Tour of Duty and returning to the states. Most of the Air Force men he met seemed to hate the assignment at Goose. Many spent their time working, eating, sleeping, drinking and, of course, complaining. That was the cycle many followed each day. There was so much to see and do at Goose that Milton didn't have a spare minute for the entire three years he spent there. That old expression "different strokes for different folks" sure applied there.

There were several learning experiences that Milton had to suffer through when he was first assigned to Goose Bay. Each midnight he would relieve a Sgt. Bowers at the hanger where they each worked six hours guarding the building. The hanger housed a small Bell Helicopter and the C-47 assigned to the Base. Often there would be a transient C-54 (DC-4) parked in the hanger.

When Milton would relieve Bowers, he would be given Flight Rations to munch on during the wee hours of the night. One night, Milton asked Bowers where he was finding the Flight Rations. "I take them from one of the air planes parked here in the hanger. No one will miss them," he told Milton.

One morning Milton finished his shift and walked over to his barracks in anticipation of sleeping through the day. Sgt. Bowers was also getting ready to go to bed. He handed Milton six Flight Rations and told him to put them in his footlocker at the end of the bunk. "My locker is full and I don't have room for them," he told Milton.

In those days the barracks were open bay, like

a long hall where everyone slept. Milton placed the rations in his footlocker and was soon fast asleep. Some time during the morning he heard a noise and slowly awoke. The sound of voices could be heard coming from downstairs in the other open sleeping bay.

Milton glanced down the stairs and observed several Officers and Non Commissioned Officers opening lockers. They appeared to be searching for something. He thought of the rations stored in his footlocker and immediately opened a window and tossed the six boxes into a ten-foot deep snow bank.

He thought Sgt. Bowers should be told that the barracks was being searched. Try as he might, he couldn't wake the Sergeant. He would grunt and roll over whenever Milton attempted to awaken him.

Soon he heard the men coming up the stairs toward his sleeping area. He scarcely was able to jump back in bed and pretend to be asleep when the men came to his cot and shook the bunk to wake him. He pretended to be slowly waking and climbed from his cot stretching his arms and yawning. The Air Police Officer, Provost Marshal and First Sergeant of the Squadron were the men inspecting the lockers.

They asked Milton to open his locker so its contents could be inspected. Milton opened the locker as instructed, and the only things in his locker were the socks, underwear and other personal items that were supposed to be kept there. After looking in his locker he was told to return to bed and they apologized for having woke him.

Milton lay in his bed observing the team attempting to wake Sgt. Bowers. It must have taken five minutes for him to sit up in bed and become aware of the people who had woke him. His locker was opened and it was stuffed full of rations, survival kits, and a small red electrician's tool box.

The Officers looked at one another and then one of them told Sergeant Bowers to get dressed because he was under arrest for stealing. He was led off to the Guardhouse. Milton was scared to death that Sergeant Bowers would implicate him, because he had been eating the rations and was storing the six rations for Bowers.

Fortunate for Milton, Sgt. Bowers kept his mouth shut. Still, Milton did a lot of sweating. That incident re-enforced the truth that stealing is wrong. Milton never forgot that lesson.

Milton discovered that the consistent loss of rations had been observed months before he was assigned to Goose Bay. The rations had been taken from the C-47's survival kits. Before any flight missing rations were always replaced. It was only recently that the survival equipment was noticed to be missing. These kits were stocked with fishing hooks, line, matches, signal mirrors and such items that would help a downed crew survive.

What accelerated the search for the ration thief

was a electrician's tool box reported missing from a desk in the aircraft hanger. Sgt. Bowers was working that night and had forgotten a letter from his girl friend. The letter was left in place of the tool box where he had been reading it. It was a stupid blunder for some one stealing something.

Sgt. Bowers was court martialed. (to non-military, that means he was tried in a Military Court) The trial resulted in him being sentenced to three months confinement and a Bad Conduct Discharge. He was to serve his time at Northeast Air Command's Confinement Facility in St John's, Newfoundland.

The story of Sgt. Bowers didn't end there. He soon escaped from the Guardhouse in Newfoundland and with a local criminal, robbed a number of stores and then the Air Police and Newfoundland Mounties cornered the two in an old farmhouse. Bowers had acquired a Thompson Submachine Gun and the two held off the authorities until they used all their ammunition and had to surrender. No one was injured, but hundreds of shots were fired – mostly by Bowers and his friend. Bowers liked to eat and the fact that he had gone without food for a long time and having run out of ammunition, led to his surrender.

He received a new court martial and was sentenced to five years and a dishonorable discharge with the time to be served in Fort Leavenworth, Kansas. The entire incident impressed Milton to no end. There were no more rations eaten by Milton while working at the hangar. It would have been a terrible thing if the C-47 would have crash-landed somewhere and the crew would discover their rations and survival equipment missing.

Those first few months at Goose Bay were action filled and quite a learning experience for young Milton.

—3—

Old Uncle Bob and Other Events

Within a month after arriving at Goose Bay, Milton had learned to use snowshoes so he could leave the confines of the roads and walk on top of the five feet of snow and through the woodlands. This freedom opened new horizons for Milton. Attempting to wade through the snow without snowshoes was an exhausting and almost impossible effort. Persons without snow- shoes would sink up to their thighs and quickly tire when attempting to wade through the deep snow.

At the bottom of the ski slope, nestled under tall Spruce trees, on the bank of a crystal clear stream was a small ten- foot by twenty-foot log cabin. The cabin was built with Black Spruce poles about eight inches in diameter. The cabin was abandoned but still furnished with a small wood stove, a table and a military style bunk along one wall. There was one small window in the end of the cabin. Most likely the cabin had been built several years before by servicemen to be used as a party cabin during their tour of duty at Goose Bay. It was a place to go to get away from the main Base. Milton decided to live there during his off duty hours. His work schedule at that time was twelve hours on duty and thirty-six hours off.

People skiing on the slope above the cabin would see smoke from the cabin's chimney and stop in to warm up and enjoy a cup of scalding hot tea or coffee, and perhaps a bowl of delicious stew made from grouse or rabbit. Often they would be so cold that anything hot would be welcomed. No one complained about the food and hot drink and kept returning.

Several of Milton's co-workers would visit during off duty hours. Soon there were two-double bunks in the cabin to accommodate the many overnight visitors. Mostly, the guests would sit and talk about the States and things they missed while assigned to that isolated and remote Base. When too many guests arrived and decided to spend the night, they would be given a sleeping bag to sleep in on the floor.

Milton spent his first Christmas Eve away from home all alone in that small cabin listening to the *Grand Ole Opry* live from Nashville, Tennessee and other American programs on a small battery operated radio that his mother and sister had sent him for a Christmas present. The Base, somehow, had a radio receiver that would pull programs in from either Canadian or American radio stations. Milton had trailed a wire from the radio through the cabin wall and attached it to the limb of a

Spruce tree to serve as an antenna and it worked. Sadly, his battery gave up the ghost toward dawn that Christmas morning. Needless to say, Milton became very homesick listening to the American radio programs.

It didn't take Milton long to locate the Hudson Bay Store where the natives purchased their supplies and sold their furs. (The Hudson Bay Company is one of the oldest corporations in the world. It was established in England to exchange supplies for furs and has been a mainstay for the natives of Canada since the sixteen hundreds. The Hudson Bay was where the first trading post was established, thus the name Hudson Bay Company)

One day when on patrol in the Air Police Jeep he stopped and walked through the Hudson Bay Store. He immediately purchased a .22 caliber Cooney brand single shot rifle for hunting rabbits and grouse. His visits to the store allowed him to observe first hand the dog teams and sleds used by the natives. They did their shopping using sleds pulled by dogs for transportation. After seeing the natives with their dogs and sleds he became obsessed with owning his own dog team. There were so many places a person could travel where jeeps couldn't go because of the snow. In the winter all the streams, ponds and rivers froze solid and became roadways. The natives could hardly wait each year until the big freeze-up.

The Base had dog kennels where several dogs

were kept by the rescue unit stationed at Goose Bay. Milton quickly became friends with several of the rescue people, including a para-rescue team consisting of four men. Milton became fast friends with those people and was always welcomed to their quarters. The rescue personnel's living quarters and dog kennels were located a good ways from the main Base.

The men at the Rescue Station discovered that Milton was interested in owning sled dogs. The Non-Commissioned Officer in charge gave him three cast-off dogs and an old sled that had seen better days to start a dog team. Milton was proud of his first dog team. The dogs were named *Slick*, *Blizzard* and *Sika*. Slick was a tall black dog. Blizzard was snow white and slim while Sika was a small, but lovable dog. He and those three dogs got along well. The smaller dog dominated both Slick and Blizzard.

The only problem was that three dogs weren't enough dog power to pull much of a load, especially in the deep snow away from the roads. Milton started seeking stray dogs during his Police patrols and "dog napping" any loose dog he could find for his team. He was bitten several times, but soon had seven dogs to pull his sled. Nobody ever complained to the Police about missing dogs.

One day he spotted and attempted to capture a large Collie. He chased it to the Base Commander's living quarters before deciding that capturing that dog wasn't too good of an idea. The dogs pulling his sled thought that catching that Collie would be exciting. Anything jumping in front of the team and fleeing always caused the team, regardless of how tired they appeared to be, to immediately become alive and start the chase. Many people in the Northland have made the mistake of fleeing from an approaching dog team, which triggers a basic instinct. Dogs have been known to attack and kill people fleeing from them, especially children and women. When a team approached, it was best to step aside and stand still until the team passed.

Milton talked to some of the Native men who worked on the Base and they demonstrated how to set snares for rabbits. Feeding his dogs had become a task that he didn't look forward to. The dogs were normally fed each evening.

Milton discovered that the Natives purchased hundred pound sacks of corn meal at the Hudson Bay Store and boiled that for dog food. Some of the natives hunted seal during the summer and stored the seal meat in wooden barrels to be used to feed their dogs in the winter. The seal meat was emerged in seal oil to prevent it from spoiling. Seal oil was the smelliest thing that Milton had ever smelled. One drop on a mitten seemed to linger forever. However, the dogs seemed to love seal meat. Milton's dog's diet was a bowl of corn meal with rabbits that had been chopped in smaller pieces, fur, bone and all, and cooked with the corn meal and added grease. He had to tend a snare line to supply the rabbits that he needed to feed his dogs. From so much practice, he became very apt at catching snowshoe rabbits with a wire snare. Sometimes, he was able to get the Base Mess Hall to save meat scraps for his dogs. That was a big help.

Training the sled dogs was a trying task. The leader was supposed to be an intelligent dog trained to respond to voice commands. Milton's first leader wasn't too smart and caused Milton much grief. One such time was when he was driving his team through the Base area and the leader took the team through an open door into the Base Exchange and one of the dogs wrapped its traces around the leg of a Colonel shopping there.

Milton was embarrassed, but the Colonel was amused by the entire incident. After he was untangled from the dog traces and the dogs removed from the Base Exchange, he ask Milton his name and introduced himself as Colonel Williams, the Base Commander. He asked Milton several questions about what he did in his spare time and how long he had been at Goose. Milton was embarrassed that he had only been there for three months. The Colonel also asked him if he hunted much and talked about grouse and rabbit hunting. Milton was impressed with the Colonel's friendliness. This accidental meeting with the Base Commander proved beneficial to Milton at a later time.

Milton discovered three other men who enjoyed

the outdoors. One day they invited him on a trip to the Traverspine River area across the river from Happy Valley. They knew a native living there. His name was Bob Michlian and he was in his seventies. His wife had died several years before and he had two grown sons and a daughter. The sons were away working most of the time and his daughter was always busy with her children and keeping house. Bob welcomed visitors from the Base. He was a veteran of World War I where he had fought with a volunteer group from Newfoundland. He never bragged, but apparently he had distinguished himself fighting the Germans and was living on a pension from the Canadian Government.

Milton visited Bob Michlian several times and became well acquainted with him. On his first visit, he and four other men had taken the worker's truck to Happy Valley and then walked the mile across the frozen Hamilton River (Churchill River now days) to Bob's home located on a point of land where the Traverspine River flowed into the Hamilton River.

The group took Bob a carton of Chesterfield cigarettes as a gift. Cigarettes only cost them $1.10 a carton at the Base Exchange Milton remembered the lunch they were served by the old man. It consisted of scalding hot tea, fresh baked raisin bread, with strawberry jam and grouse stew. In addition, he had baked several loafs of raisin bread and gave each of the five visitors a loaf to take back to the Air

Base.

After several visits to Bob's, Milton and he became friends and talked a lot. He was interested in the Southland, especially Alabama where Milton was from. He located Alabama on a map and was fascinated to learn that Alabama received little snow each year. He thought it was terrible not to have much snow in the winter. He couldn't understand how people could enjoy living in a place that didn't have a freeze-up each year. He knew that France, where he had fought in the war, didn't have a lot of snow. But after all, those people were different and it did get cold in France during the winter. Of course, the cold there wasn't anything like Labrador.

Bob told Milton about his experiences in WW I fighting the Germans in France. He had personally captured several German soldiers, including a General Officer. He opened a chest and took out a beautiful, silver clad sword wrapped in a soft cloth. The German Officer had given it to him when he surrendered. He allowed Milton to handle it. Also there were medals for bravery that Bob said little about. He was very modest.

Bob revealed to Milton that when the war ended he had arrived in St. Johns, Newfoundland in late November. The only way to return to his home at Goose Bay was by ship and already the waters were frozen and the channel wouldn't be opened until the following June. He was stuck in

Newfoundland until the ship channels would reopen. He had been away from home for over two years and he was homesick for his young wife and children.

Bob Michlian made his way to Northern Newfoundland and purchased snowshoes and other equipment, including a small toboggan for hauling his supplies. He bought three sled dogs and crossed the straits between Newfoundland and Labrador. Using a newly acquired compass to find his way, he started northwest toward home.

The trek was very difficult and after twenty days he hadn't sighted a single person. Each night he would set up his small tent and then set snares to catch snowshoe rabbits for himself and the dogs. He traveled through several snowstorms, but still kept a steady pace toward home. Often he would sight "fool hens"-a type of grouse- and shoot several for his meals.

Crossing several small mountain ridges proved difficult because of the deep snow. Some days he could travel only a few miles because of the rough terrain, but he persevered and gained more miles each day. Often he would travel until too exhausted to lift his feet with the snowshoes. On December 24th, he found himself lost on a small frozen river. As he traveled up that river, the terrain became familiar and suddenly he noticed trees that had been marked with an axe.

He realized that the marked trees were from

his own trap line. Then he recognized where he was. He had gone past the mouth of the Traverspine River and was several miles further inland and upstream. He turned and walked downstream until he reached the mouth of the river and to his home sitting on a rise above where the Traverspine flowed in the Hamilton River.

A light from a kerosene lamp radiated through a window. As he struggled up the bank from the river, the dogs tied near the house started howling and making an effort to free themselves. When he approached the door it opened and light flooded the entry-way. His wife could hardly contain herself with joy and she threw herself into his arms.

She hadn't heard from him for over a year. She had been living on supplies purchased on credit from the Hudson Bay Company Store at Northwest River the previous summer before freeze up. She was running a small trap line during his absence and snared rabbits to feed the dogs and her children. During the summer she had dried several hundred pounds of fish for her family and the dogs. For cooking oil she had trapped and killed a small Black Bear. The Christmas of 1919 was their best Christmas. His wife received the best gift of her life... her husband had returned.

—4—

Grove's Point

On a point of land where the Goose River empties into Goose Bay there was situated a nice two-story neat white house with green shutters surrounded by a white picket fence. The house looked so out of place when compared to the few other houses around Goose Bay. Milton was curious about who lived in that fine house. He heard that it even had indoor plumbing and steam heat – almost unknown to the native houses at Goose Bay.

A native, who was a friend of Milton, told him the story about the owner of the house who was getting on in years, and had lived in Labrador all his life. His name was Groves and he seldom traveled from his home because of his advanced years.

He, like most Labradorans, had at one time been poor and barely survived in that harsh climate. In those days, most families depended upon trapping and fishing for a livelihood. Wild game such as caribou, bear, seal, rabbits, grouse and fish were a main part of their diet. Food items such as flour, tea, salt and sugar was purchased from the only store within that area ... the Hudson Bay

Company Trading Post. The trading post purchased the trapper's fur each year. Fur and dried fish were the only source of income for most of the natives. Fur was the primary source.

Each family had one or more members tending trap lines in the winter. The trappers attempted to catch mink, martin, lynx, otter, fox and muskrats. The trapping areas were passed down from generation to generation. Many of the trapping areas were a long distance – by dog team or canoe – from their homes.

Small cabins were built on the trap lines. The cabins were made from logs and were about six by six foot square and five feet tall, furnished with a sheet metal wood stove. They were located a day's walk on snowshoes apart and served as overnight shelters for trappers when they were checking their trap lines. These small cabins were good protection from the harsh winter nights.

Often, after a large snowfall, the small cabins had to be uncovered so the door and stovepipe would be exposed. Milton, when traveling in the wilds, often slept in one of those small cabins that were called "tilts" by the natives. None had locks, so anyone in need of shelter was free to use them. It was proper to leave dry wood to replace the wood that a person used up during an overnight in one of the "tilts."

A home cabin was located at the end of the circular trap line. This cabin was several times larger than the "tilts." The main cabins were where the trapper stored supplies and kept his fur. Many of these main cabins were very old. Some had been built in the 1800s. Each had a loft where furs were stored and dried.

Milton had slept in some of these cabins and would spend considerable time reading the notes scribbled on the walls. He remembered one message which read, " Joe, sorry I missed you. My trapping has been good. I caught a silver fox yesterday." The note was signed, "Bill." That note was dated February 4, 1904.

The many notes written on the log walls appeared freshly written. He later discovered that the "Bill" who had written the note had been dead thirty years. He was the grandfather of the person who was presently using the cabin. Sometimes the trappers would go weeks without seeing another person. Such was the lonely life of a trapper.

During early October – before the main streams had frozen for the winter – the trappers would haul supplies to their trapping areas by canoe. In the olden days a heavy wooden dory type of boat was used. Eventually, the boats were replaced with light Indian type canoes. Each Christmas the trappers would snowshoe home to celebrate that occasion with their families. Coming home for Christmas broke up the long trapping season and was good for morale. The trapping season usually lasted from October to April.

After Christmas, the trappers would return to their areas with a small sled and one to three dogs. The dogs and sleds would be used to haul the fur and canoe back to the village when the trapping season ended. The season ended before the ice broke up and floated out.

That cycle was completed each year. Food for the dogs would be the carcasses of the fur bearing animals caught in the traps and from rabbits caught by snares. The normal trapper's diet consisted of bread cooked in an old iron skillet on top of the stove, hot tea, rabbits and "fool" hens (grouse). If the trapper could afford the extra expense, he would have several gallon cans of strawberry preserves. Strawberry preserves were the favorite of all the trappers who Milton knew.

Trapping was an important source of family income. Everything was purchased on credit from the Hudson Bay Trading Post and was expected to be paid, in full each year from the following winter's fur catch. In other words, each family lived on credit to the company store. They were almost enslaved by the company because there was no other place to sell their fur or purchase basic supplies. Occasionally, fur buyers would visit the area, but couldn't compete with the Hudson Bay Company. Most people were loyal to the "Company" because they knew it could be depended upon to be there for them each year.

Milton had to admit the Company rendered a

tremendous and valued service to the native community by being available to purchase their fur and sell them goods and equipment. Still, the families were forever in debt to the company store without any hope of ever getting ahead.

If a trapper had a bad year, – and that happened every few years – the entire family would suffer when their debt to the company store couldn't be paid and credit was cut off. If the family had a good record of paying their debt, the store would be lenient and allow basic items to be purchased on credit to carry them over until the next year, when, hopefully, the fur catch would be better.

The Groves family suffered terribly when Mr. Groves Senior drowned when his dory was swept over Muskrat Falls on the Hamilton River (Grand River). Young Groves, out of necessity, had to assume the responsibility as head of the family because of his father's untimely death. Groves was in his early teens when he became the breadwinner for his mother and three younger brothers and sisters. A good trapper was lucky back in those days to earn four to six hundred dollars a year from the sale of fur. It was a bare boned existence at best.

Year after year the Groves family barely survived. The highlight of each year was a Christmas package from Mrs. Grove's sister who resided in Montreal. Faithfully, each year the package would arrive in June on the Hudson Bay Company supply boat. The Hudson Bay boat was always the first boat in after the ice had melted from the Bay and coast. Everyone would receive nine months of mail.

One June, the Christmas gifts arrived as expected from their generous aunt. The outer wrappings, covering the brightly colored Christmas wrapping paper were Montreal newspapers. Young Groves removed the newspapers and handed each recipient his or her gift. On one of the newspapers the word "Fur Buyer" attracted his attention. That part of the paper was an advertisement from a Montreal company wanting furs to buy.

He read and reread the advertisement and could hardly believe what he was reading because the prices offered by that company was several times higher than Hudson Bay Company paid. The highest priced fur was a Silver Fox that every trapper dreamed of catching, but few, if any were caught each season. The Silver Fox was a mutation of a Red Fox that was dark black with silver tipped guard hair and was the most desired in women fashions at that time.

Hudson Bay Company offered $400.00 to $800.00 for a Silver Fox and everyone thought that to be a tremendous price and were glad to sell a Silver Fox for that amount. One of the ads from the Montreal fur buyer offered $2,800 for a large prime Silver Fox. By chance, Young Groves had caught such a fox that very season and he had yet to sell it to the company to settle his last year's debt. Red and Cross foxes were selling for $10-15 at the trading post and in Montreal they were bringing $50-60 each. Such furs were in style and in great demand by high society.

Groves was obsessed with the price list from Montreal and started planning someway to get his season's catch of fur to Montreal so he could take advantage of the higher prices. An idea came to him, why not catch a ride on the Hudson Bay's supply boat when it returned south.

He asked the manager of the company if he could work on the supply boat in exchange for a ride to Montreal to visit his aunt. The manager agreed to his request with one stipulation. That stipulation was that he could take only one trunk of clothing with him on the boat.

Graves knew that the company wouldn't allow anyone to take furs out on their ship so he had an idea. His mother had an old, but large trunk that she had owned before she had married his father. The old wooden leather bound trunk would hold a considerable amount of fur if the pelts were carefully packed.

On the evening before departure on the boat, he packed the trunk completely full of his and a few friends' most valuable furs. His friends agreed to keep silent about what he was planning. He dragged the heavy trunk aboard just before sailing and stored it below in a spot designated by the boat's Captain. The only clothing he had with him was what he was wearing. He knew it would be cold because of the ice off the coast of Labrador, so he dressed warmly with several layers of clothing. He helped load company bought fur and off load supplies at some of the coastal villages and then after a week and a half he arrived in Montreal.

Groves spent several days with his aunt and her children. He took a couple of prime fox furs to different fur buyers to determine who was willing to pay the best price. To the one buyer who offered him the best price, he confided that there were many more good quality furs to sell if a fair price was offered for the entire lot. (Sometimes fur buyers would offer a large price for one fur and then pay lower for other furs of the same quality.) The buyer paid him top prices for all his fur because Labrador fur was in great demand. (The harsh climate in Labrador causes fur to be thicker and of more value) The buyer's name was Pierre. He and Groves became fast friends. Groves received $2,100.00 for his Silver Fox pelt.

One evening when Pierre and Groves were talking, Pierre asked Groves if he knew other trappers who would be willing to sell fur to him. Groves replied that many of the Labrador trappers would sell to him for the higher price they could get and then purchase supplies from the Hudson Bay Company with the cash. The trappers had to be promised that the fur buyer would come to Labrador each year to purchase their fur.

Perhaps having a better market for their furs

could help break the credit cycle that they now lived under. Pierre asked Groves, "Why don't you buy a small boat and become a fur buyer and trader in Labrador?" Groves admitted that he didn't have near enough money to buy a boat and stock it for trading. Pierre was so interested in obtaining Labrador fur – and he was impressed with young Groves – that he offered to finance the boat and trading goods.

Groves could purchase furs from the natives and pay far more than Hudson Bay Company paid and then, sell to Pierre in Montreal for a handsome profit. An agreement was consummated between the two. Pierre loaned the money to be repaid in four years – Groves repaid the loan in two years. The boat was a very sea worthy 45' vee hull shiplap powered by a dependable diesel engine.

The venture proved profitable over the years to both persons. Groves, no doubt remembering how hard furs were to come by, always graded fairly and paid a much higher price than the company store. He was still able to earn a good profit because many of the furs he purchased were in exchange for such necessities as flour, lard, tea, sugar and other staples needed by the trappers and their families.

Groves wasn't liked by the manager of the Hudson Bay Company, but they could do nothing about his fur buying and trading. A large number of the trappers remained loyal to the company and continued to be economic slaves. No doubt remembering that the Company had existed for over three hundred years and would be around when Groves was long gone to his reward.

Mr. Groves operated his fur buying and trading business for years until he decided to retire and then he sold out to another enterprising man who failed to do as well as he had done. Mr. Groves was an old man by the time Milton knew of him. He was living comfortably in his home located on Grove's Point. He was reputed to own several apartment houses in Montreal and have over eighty thousand dollars salted away in a bank in Montreal.

He could have lived comfortably in Montreal or some other place further south where the winters weren't too harsh, but in heart, – he was a Labradoran and chose to live the remainder of his life there. He lived to well into his eighties.

—5—

Canoe Trips

Three weeks before the Korean War started in 1950, Milton and three other Military Policemen decided to take a three-day canoe trip. The plan was to follow a small stream to the Hamilton River and paddle upstream for about eight miles and camp on the far side of the river. They would be about ten miles as a crow flies from the base and any human habitation.

On May 22, the four-foot thick river ice had started melting and flowing out to the Bay. (Three consecutive years the ice starting flowing on the river on the same date.) Milton never checked to see at what time the ice started moving down the mighty Hamilton River. When the ice started moving it would pile up many feet in the air and a grinding sound could be heard as the ice crashed in jumbled piles. The forces of nature in action on the river were awesome.

When the canoe trip started there were still a large number of small sections of ice moving down stream. The water was calm and it was fun to paddle between the small and large chunks of ice floating all around the canoe. The canoe was a heavy-duty eighteen-foot craft. There was ample room for everyone aboard the canoe.

Milton insisted on tying the four-.30 caliber carbines to the canoe with shoelaces. In the event the canoe capsized the guns would be safe. To lose the weapons would result in paying for them out of already meager pay. This later proved to be the correct thing to have done as circumstances unfolded on the trip. In addition to the weapons, the canoe was carrying four sleeping bags, a small tent, food and cooking gear. Before the Korean War started Milton often checked out weapons for target practice and plenty of ammunition. On this particular trip each man was issued five hundred rounds of ammunition. They planned to do a lot of target practice.

The trip started well and everyone was enjoying the slow trip up the river paddling the canoe against the rapidly flowing current. Snow was still on the ground in the thick Spruce trees and in places ice still extended from the shore out into the water. The sky had never looked so clear and the water reflected the trees aligning the shore.

After three hours of paddling the group decided to cross the mile wide river to the far shore and travel up that side of the river. Hopefully the current wouldn't be as swift there. Soon fast moving dark clouds blotted out the sun. Without the sun the day became chilly. Once when he happened to glance over his shoulder to the rear of the canoe, he observed waves developing from the far shore of the river and moving fast toward their position. A strong wind started to gust and he could see tall waves moving in their direction. (Milton discovered when they returned to the Base that a gale force wind had also struck the Base and did considerable damage including wrecking a C-47 transport.)

He yelled a warning to the other men and swung the bow of the canoe around and toward the oncoming waves. The canoe was able to ride on the crest of two large waves and then the third wind driven wave filled the canoe completely. The men went into the ice filled water as the canoe sank under them. They grasped the sleeping bags and kept them in the water filled canoe. The canoe was constructed from wood and canvas and had no floatation provisions built into the hull.

They were about one hundred and fifty feet from shore when the waves hit the canoe. The only thing that saved them from drowning in the icy water was that section of the river was only chest deep. The far side of the river they had paddled from thirty minutes before was very deep in places. Should the canoe have been swamped there, they would have been in danger of drowning.

After the shock of the icy water, they started wading toward a section of ice protruding from the shore. The wind was howling and pushing them toward shore. One of the men was short and had to be helped along so that he wouldn't be completely submerged. The shivering men were able to climb upon an ice shelf anchored to the shore and then pulled the canoe up on the ice. Carrying all the sleeping bags and most of the provisions, they climbed the twenty some foot sandy bank and into the shelter of the thick Black Spruce trees that lined the riverbank.

The first thing that Milton did was light a large fire using the dry lower limbs of Spruce trees that he collected and piled into a large mound for a fire. He worked fast knowing they would be suffering from the wet clothing in the windy thirty-five degree temperature. He ripped several strips of Birch bark from nearby trees and using matches from his waterproof matchbox, started the fire burning. Everyone removed all of their wet clothing and helping each other, they wrung all the water they could from the clothing and then hung the wet clothing from tree limbs located near the fire.

Milton decided to check the canoe and when he looked over the bank he saw that the canoe had blown back into the water and was floating about two hundred feet downstream and fifty feet out in the river. He yelled to the others that the canoe had floated away and rushed naked back down the bank to the ice shelf and raced along the shelf until he was even with the canoe and then jumped back into the ice cold water and waded and swam to the canoe.

He grabbed the rope hanging from the canoe and started pulling it back upstream toward camp. Sergeant Fodar had followed Milton to the ice shelf where he helped pull the almost frozen Milton back up on the ice. They dragged the canoe back near their fire and tied it securely to a tree. To lose the canoe would have been serious since there was nothing but wilderness on their side of the river extending back to the James Bay. No one from the Air Base had any idea where they were. Should they have not returned at the appointed time a search would have been undertaken. No one would have any idea where to start a search. They weren't scheduled for work for two days. They wouldn't have been missed until then.

The sleeping bags were unrolled and they were pleased to find them dry inside. The men climbed into the sleeping bags and warmed up while waiting on their clothing to dry. When the clothing was almost dry Milton dressed and stood by the fire to complete the drying process. In doing this he received a steam bath after a fashion. While the other men were getting warm and their clothing was finished drying, Milton took one of the carbines and went hunting. He soon returned with three "fool hens" (A type of grouse) which he cleaned and soon had stewing in a bucket over the hot coals for their evening meal. They also had "C" rations, so there was an abundance of food.

After everyone had dried their clothing and

warm once more, they cut additional wood and erected a small tent. For entertainment they started shooting at floating ice floes about two hundred yards away. They were having an enjoyable time shooting at the ice targets when they observed a man among the ice cakes standing in a canoe waving his arms and shouting for them to stop shooting. He was among the ice floes in a direct line toward where they had been shooting.

The man was dressed in white, his canoe was white, and he had a white shield across his canoe. The purpose of everything being white was to appear like another ice floe to geese, ducks, muskrats otter, or an occasional seal. The natives would dress in white for the early spring hunting among the floating ice. They would float with the current for miles among the floes. Muskrats would often be spotted floating with the current among the ice cakes. Muskrats were easy to shoot and could be sold for one to two dollars each.

Milton became well acquainted with the man sometime after that incident and he told Milton that bullets had come so close to him that he was splashed with water and pieces of ice from the near misses. One bullet had hit the front section of his canoe. He related that he had never been so scared in his life. That was why he had taken the chance of standing up in his canoe – a dangerous thing to do in a frail Indian made canoe – to attract our attention.

Milton waved for the man to come over where they were camped. The hunter later told Milton that he hadn't cared to come to the camp, but what was a fellow to do when four men were pointing rifles in your direction and motioned for you to come to where they were. He reluctantly paddled to the camp.

He was invited up to the camp for hot tea. That he liked. He had killed several geese and an otter from his hunt. He told the men that several other natives were hunting among the ice in the river and had been scared into paddling back upstream against the current to get out of range of the rifle fire from the crazy Americans. This incident stopped the shooting at floating ice floes. After all, the men had no intention of harming anyone, mentally or physically.

After assuring the native that the shooting hadn't been directed at him, but at the ice floes, and there would be no more shooting at the ice, the man departed in a better frame of mind than when he had been summoned to the camp.

The men still had an abundance of ammunition remaining after shooting at the ice floes. Later in the day, just before dark, they starting shooting at trees. They discovered that concentrating fire on a tree could sever the tree and it would come crashing down. That worked fine until one of the men shot a tree down and it fell across the tent and fire. One man was in the tent and was trapped for a few minutes.

That tree had to be chopped through in several places to remove it from the tent and free the scared man. After that incident the shooting stopped. The man in the tent had a narrow escape and that caused sober reflections regarding the implications if the man had been killed or seriously injured. That was the last trip that members of the Air Police Squadron could check out arms and ammunition for routine camping trips. Later, as Base Scout, Milton was allowed a carbine and as much ammunition as he needed.

Another exciting canoe trip Milton enjoyed was when he crossed the Hamilton River to where a small stream flowed into the river. He had always wondered at the stream's source. He spent an entire day exploring this stream. The stream was never over twenty feet wide, but was deep in most places. He paddled, pushed, and towed the small Indian built canoe that he owned at that time up the stream to where it flowed from a small, but beautiful lake. The lake was crystal clear and had several beaver lodges located around the shoreline.

On the way up the stream, he had to drag the canoe over a fallen tree that spanned the creek. The tree protruded six inches out of the water. Traveling up the creek required three hours of rather hard work. The trip down took less them twenty minutes. That will give the reader an idea of how swift the stream flowed.

The canoe raced down the stream at a fast clip. When he approached the fallen tree, Milton dug the paddle in deep and attempted to slow the canoe, but the current carried the canvas- covered canoe over the tree trunk protruding out of the water. As the canoe passed over the log, Milton could hear a ripping sound and water started seeping into the canoe.

At the mouth of the stream, Milton pulled the half-filled canoe from the water. When he turned the canoe over he discovered a four-foot gash on the bottom of the canoe, most likely caused by a limb stub sticking from the tree that he had passed over.

The major problem Milton faced was that he still had to cross almost a mile of water to reach the other shore. At times the river could be white capping and a canoe ride across the river could be perilous. Having a severely leaking canoe made that venture impossible.

Looking around the area where he had pulled the canoe from the water, Milton discovered the area to be a perfect camping area and there were signs of previous campers, most likely Indians. He spotted several rusty tin cans. The area abounded in large Spruce trees. Many had scars from ax blows and were oozing Spruce gum.

Milton spent several minutes collecting the gum, building a fire and melting the gum. He whittled a small limb flat and used that to apply the hot rosin to the torn canvas. After the gum had cooled it provided a tight and strong seal to the bottom of the canoe. That patch job lasted for as long as Milton owned the canoe. The trip across the river and the four- mile paddle up the river to the cabin was without any problems. It was just hard work paddling against a strong current. That trip was only one of many trips made by canoe on the Hamilton River and other streams near Goose Bay.

When Milton was at his cabin located on the bank of the Hamilton River, he often had company. Canoes manned by natives would stop for what they called a "boil up." That meant having tea and food, if available. The welcome mat was always out at the cabin for anyone who desired to visit with him. After all, living alone creates a lonely person. Word soon spread and people from many different walks of life were often guests at the cabin at different times.

One Saturday the director of the Red Cross assigned to Goose, the base chaplain, Milton and an Indian family consisting of five members were seated on both sides of the large table. Only one of the Indians could speak some English. The menu for that meal was plenty of scalding hot tea, sweetened by Eagle Brand canned milk, freshly baked rolls and a large pot of porcupine stew.

The porcupine had been killed the day before when Milton was exercising three of his sled dogs. When Milton trotted up the sandy shore with three dog's leashes tied to his waist, the porcupine had suddenly emerged from the woods bordering the river. The dogs had become excited and jerked Milton off his feet and dragged him through the sand until they were able to reach the slow moving porcupine.

Each dog made an attempt to bite the porcupine and for their effort received a face filled with quills. That encounter educated the dogs that a porcupine was to be avoided. Milton had to use pliers to extract the imbedded quills from their faces. One dog had five quills inside his mouth. That dog allowed Milton to reach inside his mouth and extract the quills, one at a time, with pliers. Normally that dog would bite anyone attempting to mess with its mouth. The poor creature seemed to realize that Milton was helping it.

Porcupine meat turned dark when cooked. Adding cubed potatoes, rice, and onions, seasoned with salt and pepper made a delicious stew. There was seldom any stew remaining after a meal. Some times Milton wouldn't tell the guests what was in the stew. They ate it on faith and always seemed to enjoy what they had eaten. Some of the American guests sometimes appeared shocked when told what they had just eaten.

This particular Indian family had become close friends with Milton. He had first met them on a cold February morning. The snow was four feet deep and the river frozen solid with about as much ice. Milton was on the bank of the river chopping wood when he noticed dark objects on the ice about ten miles upstream.

He watched the objects getting closer throughout the morning. At about noon he could make out the figures of five people coming down the river. The five were on snowshoes pulling a toboggan (flat bottom sled) each and one sled dog was pulling a larger toboggan. When they approached his cabin, Milton motioned them to come up to his cabin.

The Indian family consisted of a father, mother, daughter, and two sons. The older son spoke some English. The rest of the family spoke no English. The older son informed Milton that they were hungry because their father had fallen and broken his leg the past November about one hundred miles from Goose Bay. He had just recovered sufficiently to travel on snowshoes. They had been out of food for over a month and had been living on rabbits, porcupines, and grouse.

Their family name was Semu (Some years later the *National Geographic Magazine* did a section on this family and their nomadic lifestyle) and they were seeking help. The older son indicated that he had furs to sell or swap for food. He indicated that he didn't want a handout and would swap furs for any food Milton would offer.

Milton invited the family into his cabin and started cooking a big meal for them. First of all he brewed a large pot of tea and placed it on the table with canned milk (in that Indian's language-

"Cowshooneemoo") and a bowl of sugar. Next he fried six big steaks from his Base Commissary ration, boiled potatoes, and baked hot rolls with plenty of butter and strawberry jam for a spread.

He had to admit that he enjoyed the meal too. But not near as much as the Semu family. They ate every morsel and drank the entire bucket of tea. After the meal was completed, Milton gave them two packs of cigarettes and a bag of loose tobacco for the old lady's pipe. Milton didn't smoke, but kept tobacco on hand for his guests.

The family seemed to appreciate the generous meal and to express their thanks, the young man went outside to a toboggan and returned to the cabin after a few minutes with a large canvas roll filled with fur. He offered Milton a mink and otter pelt in payment for their meal. Milton refused those valuable furs and to not insult them, took two prime muskrat pelts (valued at $1.25 each). This seemed to please the family.

The young man told Milton they had to travel further down the river and erect their tent in a good location before dark. Milton filled an old pack with food for the family to keep them alive until they could sell their furs at the Hudson Bay store and buy supplies. He gave them lard, flour, tea, sugar and two cans of condensed milk. They expressed their appreciation the best they could with the language handicap.

Later in the summer, when Milton would

return from patrol, he would often find a freshly killed grouse or rabbit cleaned and in a bucket hanging from a nail on the porch. That was one of the ways the Semu family expressed their appreciation. On occasions, the Semu family would arrive before a meal and Milton would invite them to eat. Often other people would be there for a meal, too. People from the Base would often come down on a Sunday and spend most of the day with Milton.

Milton gave Mrs. Semu several old cargo parachutes. The parachutes had been discarded by the Base and given to Milton for use in survival training. She seemed pleased with the different colored parachutes. There were white, orange, and blue parachutes. She indicated that clothing would be made from the parachutes. Milton thought that the family would have some colorful under clothing and shirts. He never discovered what she made from the discarded parachutes. She seemed to value the parachutes as a very special gift.

Before the Semus departed for their winter trapping grounds in the fall, they came by the cabin and asked Milton to paddle his canoe up river along with them and their two canoes. About a quarter mile up the river from the cabin, the Semu family had cut down and trimmed over one hundred Spruce trees for Milton to use for firewood that coming winter. All he had to do was float the trees downstream to his cabin or wait until freeze up and then sled the trees down. That was their way of repaying a kindness given to them when they were in need. This act touched Milton very deeply. They shook Milton's hand and hugged him before getting in their canoes to travel back to their trapping grounds in the interior of Labrador. They still lived the same way their father had, – living off the bounty of the wilderness.

That was the last time Milton saw the Semus because he returned to the States the following February before they came down the river for the summer. But memories of that interesting family will always be in his mind.

—6—

A Good Reason for a Revival School

January 1951 was cold and snowy, a typical winter at Goose Bay. Milton was summoned to the Provost Marshal's office where he was questioned about his activity as scout in the winter months. "Do you think a patrol around the Base is very important when the snow is so deep?" the Provost Marshal asked Milton.

He answered that there was little activity around the Base because of the deep snow and the resulting tracks would be visible. He patrolled the Base's perimeter occasionally now instead of almost every day in the summer.

In addition to his scouting duties, Milton had assisted with establishing a Survival School for the Base's few flight crews. When he was first asked to teach in the Survival School, he had demurred because of his lack of formal education. He didn't think he had the confidence to teach officers. The Provost Marshal told Milton that all he would have to do was show and tell the flight crews how to survive in a cold climate should their plane be forced down or if a crew had to bail out of a disabled aircraft into the harsh Labrador wilderness. Milton figured he could do that and thus a Survival School was born at Goose Bay.

Milton had first been approached in the fall of 1950 about starting a Survival School. Originally the school consisted of taking a few of the Base's flight crews out for a winter's camping trip. The crews were showed how to build shelters from Spruce boughs, set snares for the snowshoe rabbits, snare grouse with long limbs and a wire noose, and the proper way to protect one's self from the elements. That venture had proven very successful and the school was planning to expand and include flight crews from Westover AFB, Mass., Newfoundland and Greenland. Milton was given two assistant-volunteers and all the supplies and equipment needed to operate a school.

A paramedic team and several ground rescue personnel were assigned to Goose Bay to perform rescue missions and Milton was to be Base Scout and NCO in charge of the Survival School, and, when needed, to assist the rescue teams. Most of the rescue people were old timers who had served during World War II and many had been assigned to Bases in Greenland and Iceland in one capacity or another.

Two of those men who Milton remembers well was Gene Cooper, who married a girl from Goose Bay shortly after WW II, and Thomas E. McEvoy, who was six-foot-eight-inches tall and a knowledgeable and gentle person. He and Cooper would be available whenever Milton had too many students to handle alone. Milton was in charge of the school and those men were to take orders from him while they were working in the Survival School.

Imagine how Milton felt working with these two men. He was awed by the men's past experiences and that they out ranked him and besides, they were thirteen years older. Milton decided that he would attempt learning everything he could from those two giants in Arctic Survival experience, and, he did learn many useful things from them. Everything worked fine and they were both gentlemen in how they worked with Milton. They never tried to take advantage because of their age, higher rank or knowledge.

Milton was scheduled to attend a special Arctic Survival School in Edmonton, Alberta, Canada during February and March to help him to be a better survival instructor. That school was considered the best Survival School known. The instructors were former Royal Canadian Mounted Police personnel with backgrounds in the Arctic. Most had been Royal Canadian Mounted Police until WW II started and then they joined the Canadian Armed Forces and remained in the service after the war to operate the Canadian Survival School.

The reason for such a renewed interest in survival came about because of the large number of flight crews lost due to a lack of knowledge of survival procedures. Crashing or parachuting into a hostile and very harsh, and sometimes unforgiving terrain found in the Arctic and sub-Arctic regions by inexperienced flight crews could prove deadly. Things were much different in those days compared to the high tech of today. Downed fliers today can be quickly located and recovered thanks to satellites and homing beacons. That wasn't the case in the forties and fifties. The term "Be prepared for the worst first" was the motto of Survival Schools during that time.

There are many documented examples of flight crews that weren't prepared, physically or mentally, and failed to survive a crash or bailout where they had landed intact. One such incident occurred near Goose Bay in 1943 and can be cited as a prime example of how failure to apply survival techniques resulted in the loss of an entire crew. Similar incidents occurred throughout the world, especially as flight activity increased in the Arctic and sub-Arctic regions.

A B-26 medium bomber was being ferried from the States to England by refueling at Bases in the great circle route – Presque Isle, Maine, Newfoundland or Goose Bay, Greenland, Iceland and Scotland – carrying a crew of six. The plane approached Goose Bay during a bad thunderstorm in late August.

The plane was low on fuel and developed problems with one of its two engines. In addition to these two problems, the navigator became disoriented and missed Goose Bay completely. Seventy-five miles northeast of Goose Bay, the plane was forced to make an emergency landing when the rough running engine stopped and they couldn't maintain altitude. The pilot was able to spot an opening through the low hung clouds and made a beautiful wheels-up landing beside a lake nestled between two ridges. The plane slid to a bone-jarring, grinding halt beside the lake. The plane would never fly again even though only the engines and the bottom of the fuselage were severely damaged. No one suffered more than a few bruises and the crew quickly evacuated the plane in case of fire.

The crew had several chocolate bars and a few C- Rations. They were in shock by their situation. The tragic aspect of the entire situation was that none of the crew knew anything about survival, none were hunters or fishermen. Four of the men were college graduates and all were highly skilled in their jobs. Surviving the crash landing was a plus and after that they blew it.

One would think that everything turned out well for the crew of that B-26, but it didn't. The crash had a tragic ending that would have never occurred had they been knowledgeable of basic survival techniques. Because of a lack of survival knowledge and the will to survive, the crew slowly starved to death and as their resistance dropped because of a lack of food they were beset with colds and other respiratory ailments.

The pilot kept a log of each day's activities so when the crash site would be eventually discovered the log would reveal the fate of the crew. He listed the date each man had died and the last entry in the pilot's log was, " I'm cold and so weak that I can hardly write. Joe died yesterday and I'm too weak to bury him. I don't know how much longer I can last." That sad and despairing final entry was found in the plane beside the pilot's body a month after the date of the last entry. Each crewmember had made little or no effort to survive. Immediately after the crash two of the crew had inflated a rubber life raft and paddled upstream on a small creek in an effort to find help. They were never again heard from.

When contemplating the sad circumstance of this tragic crash, a person has to reason what would have been the crew's chances of survival should they have possessed a rudimentary knowledge of survival techniques.

The log that was so religiously kept by the pilot revealed several facts: The entire crew stayed beside the plane with the exception of the two who left by raft, and made no effort to explore their sur- roundings. Perhaps they never accepted the idea that a search plane wouldn't find them. The log revealed sighting seal in the lake – which emptied into a cove near the coast – and caribou were sight- ed on numerous occasions grazing on moss nearer than a hundred yards from the plane. There were flocks of ducks and geese on the lake and the surrounding area abounded in rabbits and "fool hens," a type of Grouse. Those animals were the food source that the natives lived on year round.

An examination of the plane revealed that a detachable .30 caliber machine gun with ammunition was serviceable and could have been used to shoot caribou, seal, ducks and geese. Flight cables and wiring from the plane could have been used for snares, parachute shroud line could have been used for fishing line to catch the abundant trout that could be seen jumping out of the water feeding on insects. There was edible moss growing on rocks along the ridge there for the gathering. "Labrador tea," a common herb grew in abundance around the lake. Birch buds and Spruce tips also would supply vitamins A and C by brewing into a tea. In other words, anyone with a bare knowledge of survival techniques could have easily survived until help arrived. The only thing the crew did correctly was drain oil from the plane to keep a fire going.

Perhaps the most tragic aspect of this situation was that a native village was located about a mile downstream from the lake. If a member of the crew had climbed to the top of the nearest ridge he would have seen smoke from the village. A crew member would have pounded on the wing of the aircraft with a rock and in the stillness of the morning or in the evening, the villagers could have easily heard the sound of pounding and would have come to investigate.

Late, in the early winter, as the snow began to accumulate, a native from the village caribou hunting discovered the crashed plane and the bodies and graves of the crew. The authorities were notified and the crash site was investigated and the bodies were removed and taken to the States for burial. The log was found beside the body of the pilot inside the aircraft. This and other similar incidents were mostly preventable and such fatal consequence cost the Air Force many top crews. It is hard to place a value on human life, but the cost of training crews is documented and can be calculated in millions of dollars. Such losses weren't acceptable when there was a simple solution and that solution was survival training for all flight crews.

—7—

Dog Team Travel and Related Events

Dog team travel was unique when compared with mechanical sleds in use at that time. The machines could seldom be depended on to operate without breaking down. Tracks and spider gears on the mechanical sleds seemed to be affected most by extreme cold and would tend to grow brittle and crack. Over the years these problems have been overcome and now modern machines are very dependable. But that wasn't true back in the early fifties.

A breakdown miles from human habitation could be devastating. Dogs didn't break down when fed and cared for properly. Many of the natives owned dog teams and they could hardly wait until winter when all the streams, rivers and lakes froze and became roadways. They hauled everything with their teams including wood.

When Milton first started collecting sled dogs, he had perhaps the worst team in that part of Labrador. When he rotated to the States three years later, he had a dog team as good as most of the natives at Goose Bay. His team wasn't that fast or powerful, but rather the dogs were in good condition from working every day. A local man named Samson Lerning who was a friend of Milton's and lived in Happy Valley owned the best dog team in the area. It was always a pleasure and perhaps a feeling of envy to see Samson working with his beautiful team. Travel by dog team required having a good lead dog. The leader had to be intelligent enough to recognize and respond to voice commands from the driver. All dogs, like all people, aren't necessarily good leaders. Leaders have to be trained. Dogs, like people, can be born with traits that help them to be good leaders.

Some of the natives actually sang commands to their dogs. Gee-gee-gee was an order to turn right and Haa-haaa-haaa was the order to turn left. "Whoa" meant to stop. No command was necessary to start the team. The dogs seemed to sense when the driver was ready. A slight movement of the sled was all that was required to get the team running.

In books and movies, the command "mush" is used to describe how the sled dogs were told to get moving. Early in the season when the dogs are fresh, they would be leaping in their traces in an effort to start. The dogs enjoyed a good run, especially with a light sled. Milton would tie his sled to a tree or other permanent anchored object with a slipknot or else turn the sled over to prevent the dogs leaving him behind. On a couple of occasions his team jump-started and took him by surprise, tossing him off the sled. He managed to grab the rear of the sled with one hand and was dragged a hundred yards before he could get the team to stop. Imagine being left behind by a dog team miles from civilization. He started tying a twenty-foot rope to the sled to be dragged behind when traveling on the open ice. If he had fallen off the sled he could have grabbed the trailing rope.

Sled dogs seem to have an almost human personality. They would often attempt to take advantage of the sled driver when he had no control over the situation. For example, once when Milton was traveling over a ten-mile-wide section of glare ice (ice without snow on the surface) which is so slippery that it is almost impossible to run with the sled, the leader failed to respond to his commands.

He was using a new dog for the leader and up to that time it seemed to have the qualities of a good lead dog. The dog seemed to realize the impossibility of Milton leaving the sled and punishing him. Instead of traveling in the direction Milton planned, the dog turned and led the team in another direction, which would eventually lead to a spot of open water on Goose Bay. Steam could be seen rising over the open water in one area of the ship channel that hadn't froze. Should Milton have jumped from the sled, he would have been abandoned miles from any shelter in the middle of the Bay.

The dogs and leader refused to stop when he yelled "Whoa" to them. They were good dogs and followed their leader as they had been trained. Milton became so desperate that he decided to shoot the leader in order to save himself and the team from a dunking in the 30- degree water and thereby regain control of the team.

He decided, before killing the leader, to shout a command to that stubborn dog and follow with a shot on the opposite side from the direction he wanted the dog to turn. After several shots, the leader turned in the desired direction and finally reached the far shore of the Bay – some eight miles – where the trail ran through the woods and through deep snow.

Milton was able to regain control and stop the team after reaching land. He gave the leader a beating with one of his snowshoes. That may sound cruel, but it was very effective in dealing with disobedient dogs. The leader underwent an immediate attitude adjustment and behaved well for the balance of the trip.

Milton replaced that dog as leader at the end of the trip. That dog became a wheel-dog – dogs hooked to the position immediately in front of the sled. He was a good pulling dog just as long as he wasn't trusted with the responsibility of leading. Some humans are like that. Being the leader seemed to go to the head of some dogs just like some people can't function in the capacity of a leader.

On another occasion, when breaking in a new leader, Milton traveled to the Mud Lake settlement down river from Happy Valley and the Base. The river had recently frozen from side to side and a traveler had to be careful when sledding over where small streams flowed into the river. These small swift streams usually froze after the river each year and the ice was thinner at that point and therefore dangerous. Often such places could be identified from the dark color of the ice. Sometimes snow would cover these areas of thin ice and create a hazardous condition that could become a death trap for the unaware.

On several occasions Milton broke through the ice and depended on his dogs to pull him from the icy water. In severely cold weather his clothing would be like a suit of armor and he would have to use a stick to break the ice formed over his knees so he could walk. He would enter the woods and build a huge fire to dry his wet clothing. Many times he would strip off all his clothing to dry before the fire. A pot of tea was brewed at the same time to warm him inside.

Milton was riding the sled behind five dogs and traveling through an inlet from Hamilton River into Mud Lake, when his leader became unresponsive and led the team through the inlet and onto bad ice. The ice section narrowed with dark open water on both sides of the ice for about one hundred yards.

The ice section finally narrowed to about three feet wide before it connected to the mainland. The sled was two feet wide and Milton was frightened by the thought of how he could swim in his heavy winter parka and clothing in the cold water. The temperature was about fifteen degrees. As the sled was pulled along the narrow section of ice, dark water was boiling up behind as the ice broke from the weight of the sled.

Fortunately for Milton, once the dogs reached land they spread out and pulled hard on the traces and the sled was pulled off the broken ice onto the land. The water in that area was very deep. That was perhaps the most harrowing experience Milton had traveling by dog sled. In situations like he experienced, the old song, "Nearer My God to Thee", took on a personal meaning.

Once on shore, he stopped, boiled tea and gave his dogs a rest. The leader appeared as scared as he was for the near escape from falling through the ice. That incident was caused by the inexperience of Milton and his lead dog. He learned from that incident. After that event, the leader – Bob – seemed to have a sixth sense in detecting thin ice and would detour questionable areas. Of course, Milton learned from that experience and was careful to watch closely for bad ice so he wouldn't be caught unaware again.

Once while traveling across a large section of ice, Milton observed a native walking toward him. One never crossed that section of ice on foot and alone at that time of the year were twelve miles of solid ice and then the river to travel up for several miles to the village.

Milton stopped and talked to the man. You just didn't ignore and pass by some one found in the middle of Goose Bay walking on the ice in mid January. The man sheepishly told Milton that he was crossing the ice between Happy Valley and the North West River Settlement by dog team when he decided to take a nap. After all, the ice appeared smooth as far as he could see, and, he was bored to death riding the sled over the vast white expansion of snow and ice.

He must have slept twenty minutes when he was suddenly awaken by a jolt and had rolled off the sled when it struck a rough ice ridge. By the time he got to his feet, the dogs, and a much lighter sled, were already a hundred feet away. The leader refused to obey the command to stop that he yelled after the retreating sled.

Next he yelled commands for a right turn in hope of the team turning in a circle until the sled approached near where he was so that the sled could be remounted. The team wavered like they were obeying, then straightened up and continued away from the man. The yelling of commands seemed to spur the team to a greater effort ... toward the opposite direction.

The man was nearer Northwest River than Happy Valley, so when Milton found him he had been walking for two hours and was becoming angrier by the moment. He told Milton that if he could suddenly locate his dogs, he would beat them to death. Milton knew the feeling from having experienced disobedient dogs. The entire episode was really very humorous from one point of view and serious when looking at the problems the man would experience if a storm blew in.

The dogs had obviously taken advantage of the man. Milton gave him a ride to Happy Valley where he later located his dogs at the home of a friend who he occasionally visited. The empty sled had arrived and his friend was in the process of organizing a search for the man. Everyone had a good laugh at the man's expense when Milton dropped him off in Happy Valley. Milton hoped the man had cooled sufficiently enough to not kill his dogs.

The best leader that Milton owned was a dog named "Red" because of his unusual coloration. This dog was a creamy white underneath with white stocking feet and a deep red over the rest of his body. His mother was a Siberian and his father a question mark.

Red was born when Milton first started acquiring dogs and he raised the dog to be a companion and a leader of the team. Everywhere Milton went, Red went. He was with Milton on many of his patrols and would alert him to anyone's presence. He obeyed and was always ready to attack any dog, wild animal, and Milton thought, a person should he be directed.

When leading the dog team, Red would not

only obey commands, but would often look back at Milton when the team came to a fork in the trail or a cross trail, and go in the direction Milton pointed, especially if Milton had been late in issuing the command. Red was the most intelligent dog he had ever owned.

Milton would brush Red's beautiful fur coat until it shone brighter than a red fox's fur. Milton was proud of Red and saddened when Red died from a distemper epidemic that swept through the area. Red was only eighteen months old and had been the best and most beloved dog that Milton had ever owned.

Red left an offspring that was black with white stocking feet like Red's, and like Red he was a good leader. He was a large dog, but not as intelligent as Red had been. Milton refused to be as emotionally involved with Bob as he had been with Red.

When leaving Goose Bay, Milton had considered taking Bob back to the States with him, but changed his mind and gave the entire team to his assistant in the Survival School – Ken Jones. The last news he had of his dog team was that they had been sent to Baffin Island to be used by a Canadian Rescue team. The memory of the dogs and dog sled travel, and especially, of Red will always be cherished.

The dog team was always a big hit with the survival students who enjoyed a sled ride and having pictures taken driving a dog team. The main function of Milton's dog team was hauling supplies for the Survival School and to transport sick or injured students back to the main road where they could be picked up by a four wheel drive vehicle.

One such incident occurred on a cold – 20 below zero – night. The Northern Lights were dancing across the frozen wilderness in an amazing display of colors. In the quietness of the night a person could almost hear a "whooshing" sound as the lights flashed across the sky. Watching the lights reminded Milton of the Indian and Eskimo superstition of the awesome Northern Lights being the wandering spirits of the dead, who were to roam the night skies for eternity.

One of the survival students complained of a shortness of breath and a severe pain in his side. The survival camp was located on a chain of lakes on the far side of Alexander Mountain, northwest of the Base. The radio that Milton had for contact with the base failed to operate properly (probably because of the Northern Lights) and he couldn't contact the Base. The sick man revealed to Milton – when he was visited in the hospital the next day – that he had never been so scared in his life as he was when hauled from the lakes to the main road by dog team.

When the dogs were well rested and it was night time, they seemed to have more pep and were willing to run faster than during the day when hauling a heavy load.

To reach the main road required traveling the length of a small lake, following about a mile of trail cut through the woods to another lake and then down that lake to an old logging trail that led to the main road. The trail between the lakes was a winding trail with many sharp turns that followed the contour of the land between the lakes. Milton had cut this trail for the purpose of hauling supplies with his dog team.

The sled often bumped into and scraped trees and, on occasions almost turning over, as Milton guided it through the woods at a fast clip. The dogs set a record time for traveling the last mile of the trail. The man was wrapped in a sleeping bag and tied into the sled. Every time the sled's bumper would scrape or bounce off a tree or the sled tilted dangerously on its side when covering that rough terrain, he would yell, moan and groan. He never knew when the sled would plunge off the side of a hill or into a ravine. He was absolutely terrified.

When Milton finally reached the road on top of Alexander Mountain, he could see the control tower and Base lights in the distance. However, try as he might, he couldn't contact the Base. The man in the sled was still scared and moaning when a jet fighter flew overhead on a night intercept mission.

Milton was able to contact the F-94 pilot. And he relayed a message to the Base Hospital to send an ambulance to the mountain to pick up the sick man. The man was admitted to the hospital with a gallstone attack and was able to return to the States for an operation.

He informed Milton that if he had realized how hazardous the dog sled ride would have been, he would have rather endured the pain than experience the sled ride through that rough terrain. That was an experience he would always remember.

—8—

The Goose Bay Survival School

Milton had been ordered in late 1950 to locate a site and establish a Survival Training Camp. He selected an area in a frozen bog below the Base's water pump station. This area was near the Base, requiring only fifteen minutes of travel from the classroom to the site. The officer in charge of survival was Capt. Raymond Rose from New York City. He had no survival experience and was only a figurehead to satisfy the requirement that an officer be available to deal with the officers attending the Survival School.

Each student was issued one package of inflight rations per day. The ration was a military ration designed for one meal. The students had to make do with the one ration by supplementing it with any game they could capture. The classroom portion of survival training consisted of signaling and basic survival concepts. In the bush portion of the survival training, students were required to construct a shelter from Spruce boughs, build a base for a fire in the deep snow and then attempt building a signal that could be seen from the air identifying that they were stranded and needed help.

Basically, the student was to acquire a feel of what it was like to be stranded and have to live with what they had with them. Also, students were taught how to protect themselves from frostbite, freezing and to secure wild game. It was a new experience for most aircrew members. For those disliking cold weather it was an ordeal.

Since Milton and Captain Rose planned to be in the area all winter, Milton erected a para-tepee. This shelter was made similar to the Indian tepee. A framework of poles was erected and covered with a parachute. In addition, a small sheet metal stove was installed. This type of stove was widely used by natives in the northern woodlands.

The stove was about the size of a large boot box. A three-inch diameter pipe was attached to the stove and ran through a hole cut in the parachute. When stoked with a few sticks of dry wood the stove would get red hot. The tepee would be comfortable as long as wood was fed into the stove.

The first day of survival training at that site went well. The twenty students erected lean-to shelters made from Spruce boughs and cut a good supply of wood to last the night. Milton spent the entire time circulating from shelter to shelter instructing and assisting the students with building shelters and giving tips on such things as packing the snow and building a platform for the campfires so that the fire wouldn't sink into the snow and be extinguished. The snow was over four feet deep. Also, he showed members of each team how to set snares for rabbits, squirrels, grouse, and to identify certain scrubs, tree buds, and bark as a source of food.

At the end of the day, Milton was tired and ready to retire. He and Capt. Rose spread their sleeping bags over a deep carpet of Spruce boughs worked into a thick mat for a cushion from the ground. Prior to building the para-tepee, Milton had dug down to bare ground. The tepee wasn't completely finished because of the time spent preparing the students for the night. There was a slit about twelve inches wide from floor to top left open. When they retired the temperature was about twenty degrees and they found the double eider down sleeping bags more than ample for a comfortable sleep.

Milton woke at first light and discovered that it was snowing and the tepee was filled with snow. Their sleeping bags were covered and even the stove had to be dug out in order to start a fire. Capt. Rose wasn't too happy about awakening in the cold and snow.

After Milton had a fire kindled and most of the snow shoveled out of the tepee, Capt. Rose got up, dressed and asked Milton to please harness the dogs and give him a ride to the pump house where he could use the phone and call for a ride back to his base quarters.

He told Milton, "The survival school is yours. You run it like you want and each Saturday before the students are scheduled to leave camp, I will ride out in the Base helicopter and bring everyone steaks and apple pie." That was the one and only time Capt. Rose spent a night in the Survival Camp.

Often there would be over thirty students camped at one time who were divided into small groups. Most were eager to learn, but some attempted to cheat and take survival training lightly. Any student caught with food other than what was issued was reported to Capt. Rose and they failed the school.

Everyone was informed in advance what was expected so those who cheated were without excuse. Milton once discovered two bottles of wine in one of the camps. He confiscated the wine over the protests of two officers. He tossed the wine bottles into a snow bank next to the tepee and during the night the temperature dropped so low the wine froze. That was a cold night! The men's Commander was attending the school at the same time and he told Milton that he would "take care" of the two officers who had smuggled the wine into the camp when they returned to Newfoundland.

The workload and constant pace became a grind and Milton was loaned two Sergeants from the Rescue Squadron assigned to Goose Bay. These two men were experts in Arctic survival and had been assigned to Greenland during World War II and once before to their present assignment, Goose Bay.

One of the men was soon to depart for the Antarctic for an assignment with a team to explore a section of that desolated land. His name was Sergeant Thomas McEvoy and the other Sergeant was Gene Cooper. Milton had worked with them before and had learned much from that association. They were a tremendous asset for the three weeks they were available to assist with the survival training.

Milton issued one shot gun to each team to secure wild game to supplement their diet. He would take a team out for a hike on snow shoes through the woodland and show them the best places to set snares for rabbits and where to look for "fool hens"(a type of grouse). For many, using snow-shoes was a new and tiring experience. Milton always marveled at the ease of travel on top of four or five feet of snow using snowshoes.

Once he had made a trip in the early spring by dog team out to an island in Goose Bay. The snow was frozen hard and snowshoes weren't needed. While on the overnight fishing trip the temperature increased to above freezing and the snow became soft. The dogs were having a difficult time pulling the sled and Milton attempted to walk on the thawed snow and at each step would break through up to his thighs.

Progress was so slow that an extra day of travel was required for the return trip. Fortunately, the temperature dropped during the final night of that trip and he was able to complete the long trip back to his cabin while the snow was crusted. He had a sled load of trout, smelt, and cod fish. After that experience he was never without snowshoes whenever he traveled in the winter.

He demonstrated to the students how to take turns breaking trail so they wouldn't tire too quickly. Since a downed crewmember wouldn't have snowshoes, the students were taught to make emergency snowshoes from tree limbs and parachute shroud lines.

The first year's Survival School was a success and was to be expanded the following year to include more aircrews from Newfoundland, Greenland, and Westover AFB, Mass on a regular basis. Captain Rose returned to the States as soon as his one-year tour was completed. He had been a good person to work with.

Before he rotated to the States, he asked Milton to take him on a dog sled trip to Northwest River. This was a settlement east of Goose Bay. They met a Dr. Patton, the only doctor, other than military doctors, in that entire region. They enjoyed a delicious meal of baked beans and biscuits with Dr. Patton. They spent the night in the attic of the home of a native family with whom Milton had become acquainted. The family rented their attic to travelers and charged one dollar per night. They kept apologize for charging. Milton knew that they needed the money and he thought that the charge of one dollar was very generous on their behalf. The woman who kept house was married to a Newfoundlander who was employed on the Base. They had four children and he seldom came home. The house belonged to her father. She was always hungry for news from the Base and her husband. Every time Milton traveled to Northwest River he would rent the attic room.

Then, there was the long dog sled trip back to Goose Bay the following day. They had to contend with a fresh snowfall that made travel slow and difficult. When they finally arrived back at Goose Bay, Capt. Rose told Milton that he would never take such a trip again, but would cherish that experience for the rest of his life.

Milton decided to move the Survival School to Alexander Mountain Northwest of the Air Base. A chain of eight small lakes was situated to the rear of the mountain. These lakes were located northwest of the Base. The plan was to rotate the campsites along the shore of each lake so that there would always be virgin territory for the survival camps. A camp in the same spot each week would scare away any wild game and soon deplete dry firewood.

When winter arrived in a fury of storms and

cold temperatures, it was time for the winter phase of the Survival School to start. The first class met in early November after the ice on the lakes was at least a foot thick and would continue until early May.

The new officer assigned to supervise the Survival School was a Lt. Enes. He was a medical officer and had never hunted for game or camped out a single night in his life. He was strictly a city boy from a large city in Pennsylvania. He didn't care for the assignment, but he had to obey the orders of his superior. His presence satisfied the requirement that a commissioned officer be present and in charge.

He told Milton that he intended to remain by a warm fire and was only to be bothered in the event of an emergency. There were no emergencies that year in the Survival School, so he wasn't bothered. Milton ran the school successfully and enjoyed the opportunity of teaching others survival skills.

Some people, it seems, would have a difficult time surviving regardless of how much survival training they were given. Some of the Flight Crews would sit around their campfire wrapped in sleeping bags and would only become involved when urged. Perhaps they thought sitting around the fire for four days and nights was all that was needed to pass the Survival School. The real test of what they learned from the school would be, God forbid, if and when they crashed or had to bail out over the Arctic.

That would be a test that one either passed or failed. There would be no in between. One either lived or died. Many unprepared people had died because they had underestimated the dangers of the Arctic. The Arctic is unforgiving to the unprepared.

Once when a new class started their four days and nights of survival living, Milton circulated from camp to camp to render whatever assistance needed. When approaching one camp he heard swearing before walking into that camp. He observed one man attempting to light the end of an eight-inch in diameter green Spruce log. The man had exhausted all the match supply issued to his camp. When matches are limited in supply, the waste of matches could mean life or death in an actual survival situation.

His futile effort revealed clearly that team hadn't paid attention to the class room instruction about starting fires. The lower limbs of Spruce trees all around that camp had moss hanging from the sheltered lower tree branches and it was dry. In the immediate area were several large Birch trees with loose and very dry bark. Milton re-instructed the men on fire building. He ripped several pieces of birch bark from a nearby tree and broke several small dry limbs from a Spruce tree and soon had a large fire burning.

They thanked him profusely for the help rendered because they had started to become cold and realized that a fire was a necessity. Thereafter, they were all ears whenever Milton offered advice.

Another camp team consisted of complainers. Each team had been issued a 12-gauge shotgun for hunting. No one from that camp had ventured over fifty feet through the deep snow from their shelter seeking game. When Milton stopped by that camp to see if he could be of assistance, he was greeted by complaints. The main issue was that they had spotted no game and they were hungry. The one small meal issued per man, which was to last the entire day, had been eaten and now evening was approaching and they had nothing to eat.

Milton observed bird droppings next to where the men were seated on a log by the fire and glanced skyward spotting five "fool hen" (grouse) roosting on a limb of a large Spruce tree above where they were camped.

"Hand me your shotgun," Milton told one of the officers. "Is the gun loaded?" he asked the man.

"Sure, but there is nothing to shoot," he replied.

Milton took the .12 gauge pump Winchester shot gun and succeeded in killing three of the grouse before the remaining two flew to safety.

One of the grouse fell at the feet of the man who had complained most. It almost hit him when it fell. Milton handed the shotgun back to the man, picked up one of the grouse for his dinner and departed without saying a word to them. Thereafter that team spent more time hunting and less complaining. They made a welcomed and delicious stew from the two grouse.

After the training was completed they came to Milton and apologized for their initial bad behavior. They told Milton that was the best trick ever played on them; they had noticed grouse dropping on the edge of their shelter after Milton had departed.

That had actually been a valuable lesson. Everyone enjoyed a good laugh about the incident and thereafter when Milton visited one of the camps, the first thing the men would do was look up in the trees to see if there were grouse sitting over their heads. Once, one of the men spotted a red squirrel that they weren't aware of and shot it. They stewed the squirrel for several hours and it remained tough. But, it was better than nothing. (The Arctic Red Squirrel is taken for its fur.)

Lt. Enes didn't last too long as the officer in charge of the school. He was soon replaced by a 2nd Lt.LaRochelle, who had just graduated from college with a ROTC commission. He was a former marine and had obtained the rank of Private First Class for the three years spent in the marines. He was a different officer than the other officers. He wanted everything to operate by the book. Everything had to be done a certain way... his way, right or wrong. One thing to his favor was that he had been raised in upstate New York and therefore wasn't a stranger to snow conditions.

Milton had been assigned an instructor assistant. His name was Corporal Ken Jones. Ken was a likable sort, who always smiled and maintained a positive attitude regardless of how difficult things became. He was a tremendous asset to the Survival School. He was learning survival by a hands on experience. He and Milton got along well and enjoyed teaching and living survival. He could always be depended on to do a good job with whatever task he was assigned.

Jones noticed that officers attending the school referred to Lt. LaRochelle as "Rocky." That officer always called Jones "Casey." Once when Jones and LaRochelle were working together, Jones addressed LaRochelle as "Rocky" and in turn received a severe reprimand. He was told that even when alone, Jones would always address him as Lt. LaRochelle. This rebuke hurt Ken's feelings in that he was just trying to be friendly when they were alone together and would have never addressed him with such familiarity in the presence of other officers.

Prior to the advent of 2nd Lt. LaRochelle, each survival student carried his own equipment to the survival site. LaRochelle decided that since Milton had a dog team and sled, he would haul the officer's food and sleeping bags to the campsite. Milton disagreed with that order, but had to obey since he was only a SSgt and worked for the officer.

Before this, a student carried everything he would use in a pack and walked on snowshoes for the experience. Now Milton was required to haul the supplies and equipment to each camp and pile the items in front of that site. He named this the "Pile System." This required two trips into the survival area with a heavily loaded sled. That took way from the actual time normally used in assisting the students with preparing for their first night.

The survival camp was located on the third lake behind Alexander Mountain. On a small island connecting the third and fourth lake a small cabin had been built years before by trappers or fishermen. LaRochelle decided that the instructors would live in that cabin. Normally, Milton and Jones would live in a small wall tent that was easy to heat and proved to be comfortable in the coldest weather.

Living in the cabin required cutting a large amount of firewood to keep the large stove burning and the cabin warm. For two weeks, Milton and Jones spent considerable time cutting wood when they should have been tending to their students. 2nd Lt. LaRochelle wouldn't assist with any of the work because he was an "Officer and Gentleman". He spent considerable time in the cabin feeding the wood stove the precious supply of dry wood provided by Milton and Ken Jones.

Finally, after a difficult day working with thirty-five students, Milton and Jones returned to the cabin and LaRochelle informed Milton that most of the wood was burned and that he and Jones should start cutting more wood for the night. This was the straw that broke the "camel's" back. Milton politely informed 2nd Lt. LaRochelle that officers and enlisted men shouldn't be sharing the same living quarters. Furthermore, he and Jones were going to move out of the cabin and into the wall tent. They were too busy tending to the needs of the students to cut wood to fuel the large stove in the cabin.

The Lt. protested, but Milton was firm regarding his resolution to move into the tent. He and Jones took their sleeping bags and other equipment and erected the small six by ten-foot tent. Soon the tent was warm and they were cooking their evening meal on the small sheet metal stove.

For several hours each day, they could hear Lt. LaRochelle chopping firewood to maintain the wood stove in the cabin. He never forgave Milton for insisting on moving to the tent. Milton didn't care how the Lt. felt about the situation. After the way he had treated Ken Jones, Milton felt it would help the Lt. stay in good physical condition by cutting his own wood.

The students spent considerable time practicing signaling passing planes. They learned to use signal mirrors, flares, and using Spruce boughs, laid out in a large S O S and X in the snow. (These signals meant that an emergency existed or help was needed). Also dead wood was piled in one spot to be lit as a signal fire in the event a plane would pass over. All of this effort was necessary to aid search parties in locating downed fliers.

Since the lake where the Survival School was located was behind Alexander Mountain northwest of the Base, the Base's radar was unable to pick up aircraft that flew over the camp at a very low altitude. Many of the students were fighter interceptor pilots who took great pleasure buzzing their friends who were undergoing survival training.

Once, while giving instructions on the lake, Milton glanced over his shoulder and observed a F-94 fighter flying about fifteen feet above the lake ice and approaching them. (The lake was only about two hundred feet wide) He yelled a warning to the other students who immediately fell to the ice as the plane flew over them.

Near the end of the lake was a small island with trees protruding forty feet in the air. The plane had to turn on its side with a wing almost touching the ice to fly between the island and the hill at the side of the lake. The smell of jet fuel covered the training site on the ice after the plane flashed past at considerable speed. A Colonel attending the school muttered "crazy fool" as the plane did that tricky maneuver.

Later Milton discovered the pilot was Lt. Fritz, who was born in Germany and was impressed with the American fighters flying over when he was a young teen during World War II. He aspired to be an American fighter pilot and when his family moved to the U.S. and became citizens, he joined the Air Force and became a fighter pilot. Everything was a fulfillment of a dream for him. Milton had him as a student and his friends did their best to repay for the buzz job. The class had to leave the open lake ice because of the frequent buzzing by planes.

Later in the summer, Lt. Fritz flew to Newfoundland and landed during a heavy fog. Ground approach radar was located in a small two-floor shack near the runway. Something was wrong with the radar that foggy day and Lt. Fritz landed beside the runway on grass and plowed through the ground floor of the Ground Approach Radar site.

Fortunately for the GAR crew, they were all in the second floor of the building when Lt. Fritz was suddenly under them in his F-94 fighter. He destroyed the site and the F-94. No one received a scratch from that accident. He was lucky to have walked away from such a crash. The last that Milton heard of Lt. Fritz was that he had been reassigned to Westover AFB, Mass.

Teaching survival was a dream for those enjoying the outdoors. Sleeping under the stars that appeared large enough to reach up and touch, and then to see the Northern Lights flashing across the sky in living color was an experience to cherish. Unless one has lived in that land, it is difficult to appreciate the stark beauty of the North Country.

One January day when the dog team was loaded on a truck for the trip to the trail that would lead to the survival site, a Captain Peterson, who identified himself as being from the Office of the Director of Training for the Northeast Air Command, approached Milton. He told Milton that he was to live with him for four days and experience everything that was required in operating the Survival School.

Milton politely told the Captain that he should obtain Lt. LaRochelle's approval because he was in charge of the Survival School.

"Lt. LaRochelle is only a figurehead to satisfy the requirement that an officer be assigned to the school. You are the one who operates the school."

Milton didn't know what to say and only replied, "Yes Sir."

Milton informed Lt. LaRochelle that an inspector from Northeast Air Command was to accompany him to the survival camp and evaluate how the school was operated. LaRochelle became visibly upset and demanded from the Captain that everything should go through him.

He and the Captain talked for a time in private and LaRochelle said nothing further to Milton. However, he spent more time with the students that time out. And, instead of chopping wood during the day, he could be heard chopping wood for his cabin after dark. He spend more time circulating from camp to camp than ever before.

"Forget I'm here. Continue to do what you would do if I wasn't here," Captain Peterson informed Milton.

"I want you to capture some wild game, maybe a grouse or rabbit and prepare them for our meals," he stated.

Snaring a rabbit wasn't any big problem because he had a large snare line to help feed the sled dogs and to donate to the survival teams. However, the grouse were more difficult to locate. The Captain followed him around on snowshoes when he made his rounds to the camps assisting with preparation for a night that promised to be well below zero.

There was always a concern of frostbite. The men carried signal mirrors that could be used to look for yellow spots on their faces that indicated frostbite. The students were taught to look out for each other and warned of the dangers of frostbite. Seeing the students often peering into mirrors might make someone think they were vain and concerned with their looks. Using the mirrors helped detect frostbite in sub zero weather and allowed time to take protective action before severe damage occurred.

Milton and Capt. Peterson snowshoed through the woodland near the camp seeking game. Milton spotted two grouse in a tree immediately ahead of them. Instead of shooting the grouse, he decided to show off his skills.

He cut a long pole. To the end of the pole he attached a noose made from copper wire. Whispering to Capt. Peterson to remain behind a large Spruce tree, he approached the grouse that were roosting on the lower limbs of a Fir tree, taking care to keep a large tree between himself and the grouse. He reached around the tree with the eight-foot pole and jerked the noose over the head of one of the grouse. The other grouse flew higher into another tree.

Milton approached that grouse using the same ploy of hiding behind a tree, reached around the tree and threw his small hatchet knocking that grouse off its perch on the tree limb. The reason that he was able to accomplish this feat was because he had discovered that when the day was cold and still, the grouse weren't much wilder than chickens. (Probably the reason they were called "fool hens".) But, when the wind was blowing they were as wild as a covey of quail. He used this knowledge when hunting the "fool hens". This grouse was the size of a Cornish game hen and delicious, fried, baked or stewed. Milton ate many grouse while stationed at Goose Bay and never grew tired of their flesh.

Later he took Capt. Peterson to his snare line and located five rabbits that were caught in the snares. Once back in camp, he lit a fire in the small tent stove and started cleaning one rabbit for dinner and the two grouse. He again showed off somewhat by cleaning the birds and rabbit without using a knife. That seemed to impress Capt. Peterson very much.

Milton fried the birds and stewed the rabbit. The Captain wasn't too hungry after watching the game being cleaned and then cooked. He did eat some of the grouse and declared it good. "Milton, survival seems to come easy for you," the Captain stated.

At the end of the week of observing the Survival School in operation, Captain Peterson thanked Milton for his patience in showing how the survival school operated and said he was greatly impressed with the school and how survival was taught. He went on to say how impressed he was with Milton and Corporal Ken Jones because of the effort they exerted in teaching the students survival tactics. He then informed Milton that in the immediate future there would be an Air Force film crew making a training movie of the Survival School. In later years Milton was able to view that movie.

Perhaps there was some fun in survival training for the students also. On the second day of survival, when everyone was settled, the students would often ask to have a picture taken of them driving a dog team or riding on the sled. Hundreds of pictures were taken of the dog team and students.

One picture of Milton and his team was blown up to a four by six-foot size and placed in the Base Terminal. Milton visited the terminal a couple of times to view the picture of him and the dog team. Seeing his picture posted in the Flight Terminal was almost sufficient to give him a swelled head.

Sharing the wall in the terminal with Milton's picture was that of Ellen, the only WAF assigned to the Base at that time. She was the Base Commander's secretary. She made TSGT in a very short time and eventually married a Capt. Freeman, who served as the Air Police Officer.

Being the only WAF assigned to the Base at that time made her almost a mascot. Everyone loved her. She possessed a good "all American girl appearance and personality." She lived in a room in the dorm where the few civilian women assigned to the Base lived.

Mid-January was Milton's last day operating the Survival School. Several enlisted men and two officers with considerable experience were assigned to the Base and took charge of the school and were expanding it to train SAC personnel from several Air Force Bases in the States. Ken Jones had time remaining on his tour of duty, so he would serve as instructor until he rotated to the States. The school was expanded to include both summer and winter survival. Something that Milton had wanted to do, but was unable because of his scout duties, There just wasn't time to do everything that needed to be done.

Major. Willie Knutsen and Capt Adamson were the officers assigned to operate the school. Both had considerable Arctic experience. Willie Knutsen had been raised in Greenland and had parachuted into Norway during World War II to harass the

Germans. Apparently, he had done a good job. Obviously, he had been good at what he did because he had survived to tell about his experiences. He had lived in the mountains and traveled on skis in the winter. Milton wished that he could have remained at Goose Bay and worked for that gentleman.

A good book could have been written about the exploits of Willie Knutsen. Finally the school was staffed with officers that were experienced and motivated. Second Lt. LaRochelle was relieved of his position and reassigned to a job more fitting his rank and experience.

—9—

The Canadian Survival School

Milton flew to Westover AFB, Mass in January of 1951 on the Base's old C-47 Gooney Bird and then boarded and rode a train across country to Great Falls, Montana where he was to be scheduled for a flight to Edmonton, Alberta on an Air Force plane.

The Base at Great Falls was located in a very scenic area and was extremely cold and little snow was on the ground. In the distance he could view a panorama of beautiful snow capped mountains with a bluish tint. He had never seen anything as awesome as that area.

The transient barracks was a World War II building with a single pot bellied coal-burning stove positioned in the center of the building. The temperature had dropped so low that several men sat and napped the entire night wrapped in blankets around the stove. They kept the stove red-hot and as long as a person was near the stove he would be comfortable. The men sleeping in the extreme ends of the barracks slept under several blankets and in all their clothing. The only insulation between the men and the cold was one-inch boards and an asphalt siding. That January night was one of the coldest on record in Great Falls.

Morning slowly came and the temperature warmed considerably as the sun made an appearance. Milton walked toward town – located a short distance from the main gate – to a restaurant and ordered coffee, ham and eggs. The breakfast was delicious and cost ninety-five cents. He paid for his breakfast with a ten-dollar bill and received change consisting of a nickel and nine silver dollars.

At that time a large amount of silver was being mined in Montana and silver dollars were used by most businesses instead of one-dollar bills. Milton planned to keep his silver dollars as a souvenir but once he reached Edmonton, Alberta where the school was located they were quickly spent. Money was a thing that Milton had little of and had a difficult time keeping what he had.

After two days a C-47 flew Milton and several men who were from other bases to Edmonton. The classroom portion of the school was held at a Royal Canadian Air Force Base. This part of the training dwelt with various means of signaling and procedures to follow when you were suddenly downed or bailed out in the Arctic. Two weeks were spent learning these techniques in the classroom.

Training for surviving in the bush would be taught under actual survival conditions at Fort Nelson, British Columbia and after that segment was completed, they would be flown to Cambridge

Bay, Victoria Island, located north of the Canadian mainland in the Arctic Ocean. There, they would receive barren land survival training with Eskimo instructors and actually spend a few nights under barren land survival conditions living in igloos that they were to construct.

After successfully passing the written test in Edmonton, Milton and fourteen other students were flown to Fort Nelson, BC for participating in the woodland part of survival training. They arrived in early afternoon and were issued special Arctic clothing to test, sleeping bags and rations for six days. The rations consisted of a tuna size can of meat, a chocolate bar, tea and crackers. Normally three of the ration would be issued to Canadian Air Force Personnel per day. For survival purposes only one ration was issued per day or roughly one third the normal ration needed to sustain a person living in that cold temperature. (The recommended diet for Arctic outdoor living is a minimum of 6,000 calories.)

The students were hauled by truck twenty miles up the Alcan Highway and met there by an Indian instructor named Alex. A narrow trail led from the highway through a thick forest of Spruce and Fir and deep snow requiring the use of snowshoes. Several types of snowshoes were available for issued and Milton quickly accepted a pair of long Objibway snowshoes five feet long and turned up on the ends. He had used that type of snowshoe almost daily in Labrador.

The camp – previously built by other survival students – consisted of Spruce bough lean-to shelters open at the top with a small entryway on the sheltered side. The temperature had dropped to over twenty below zero but there was no wind to cause severe chilling. Carrying the heavy packs and dressed in the new coveralls they were testing kept the students warm.

Once they arrived at the camp they were introduced to the four instructors. Two were former Royal Canadian Mounted Policemen and two were Cree Indians. The instructor's shelter consisted of a large tent positioned on a wooden frame. A large wood burning stove was used for cooking and heat. Next, the students were divided into teams of five men and shown the brush lean-to they would call home for a week. For some team members it would prove to be a long and very cold week. Imagine what it would be like to find your self cast suddenly into the outdoors in sub zero weather. Most people aren't prepared for such a drastic change.

Milton was fortunate to be assigned to a team with two other Americans and two Canadians. One of the Canadians was Squadron Leader Murray– about the same rank as an Air Force Major. Milton will never forget that gentleman. He was a friendly sort and wise to the Arctic after spending years as a fighter pilot in various areas of the North Country. He felt that he, too, needed to sharpen his survival skills since he flew often. Each team had been left to apply the knowledge learned in the classroom to actual survival hands-on experience.

When his team was assigned to a lean-to, Milton noticed, as they walked to their shelter a rabbit trail, six inches deep from consistent use, crossed past the back corner of the shelter. That evening after helping cut a good supply of wood and hopefully enough to keep the fire burning all night, Milton set two copper wire snares in the rabbit trail. He didn't mention to the other members of his team what he had done. When outdoors, he always carried several rabbit snares in his pocket as well as matches in a waterproof container. He considered those items as an insurance policy against going hungry and being cold.

In the chilly darkness of evening the men sat around the brightly burning fire and started to eat their small can of meat and chocolate bars. Before the men actually started eating, Squadron Leader Murray told the team that he had a proposal to make. He stated that the team members could do what they wanted, but please allow him to inject his views regarding the situation. He proposed that the team pool all their rations and use the meat to make a stew by adding water from melted snow to make the meat go further.

Also, he recommended that the team make hot chocolate from the chocolate bars in a common pot. That way throughout the day there would always be a hot liquid to drink. SL Murray suggested that the team could have a light meal for breakfast and lunch while having a hardy meal of stew for dinner. Everyone agreed that his ideas were good.

His next suggestion caused several people to glance at each other. He wanted to zip all five sleeping bags together and four men sleep at a time. The night would be divided into watches to keep the fire going and prevent sparks from burning the team's clothing or sleeping bags. Everyone agreed, however, some reluctantly, perhaps thinking that sleeping with strangers in one large sleeping bag was a somewhat different situation than they were accustomed. The temperature was expected to drop to fifty below zero that night. Actually the temperature dropped to fifty-six below zero.

Squadron Leader Murray reasoned that if everyone received a good night's rest they would be able to cope with short rations and the extreme cold. Few of the team members had ever camped under severe cold and deep snow conditions.

The first night everyone in Milton's team slept warm and mostly comfortably. During the night when one person would turn over everyone would automatically turn over. It didn't take long at all for the team to adjust to the sleeping arrangements. Milton was impressed with how SL Murray had organized the camp. He never made an effort to force his views on the team. All of his recommendations were just that – recommendations. But they were so practical that each team member was willing to follow Murray's instructions, and his suggestions turned out to be an excellent solution to cope with the cold and shortage of food.

The other two survival teams did everything as individuals; ate their individual rations, complained about cutting wood and about who would feed wood to the fire during the long night. Late at night when Milton had fire guard, he could hear grumbling from the other camps and activity. Apparently someone would get cold and finally get up and cut wood. It was Milton's opinion that members of the other two camps acted like spoiled brats.

As the temperature dropped, the other teams would sit by their fires wrapped in sleeping bags in an effort to stay warm and doze. Often, they ate their meager rations for breakfast and went hungry for the rest of the day. Milton's team could almost feel sorry for the other team's plight, as they had the same opportunities, but refused to cooperate with each other as Milton's team had.

The first thing Milton did after breakfast the morning after arriving at the camp was to check the rabbit snares he had set the night before. The snares had captured two large Snowshoe rabbits.

When he (rather proudly) took the rabbits into the shelter, his team immediately voted Milton to be the camp hunter and excused from all other duties.

Milton's assignment each day was roaming the woodland around the camp snaring rabbits and shooting fool hens (grouse) for the team's stew pot. He was given the .22 caliber single shot rifle assigned to each team for hunting wild game.

One of the rabbits was cleaned immediately and added to the stew pot for that evening's dinner. The other rabbit was hung on a tree limb until needed. The stew emitted a delicious aroma that could be smelled all over the camp. Other team members "just happened" to stop by for conversation at dinner time.

Most of the other teams had already eaten their rations that morning and were genuinely hungry. They wanted to know what was cooking that emitted such an aroma. After the team had eaten their fill of ration meat and rabbit stew, the remainder was shared with those who came visiting and had just "happened to bring their tin cup with them." Combining the ration meat and rabbit gave a wonderful flavor. Perhaps being hungry as the men were made any type of food smell good.

The daily effort in hunting grouse and running the snare line allowed Milton to become familiar with his surroundings and provided a valuable addition to the stew pot. After a few days of Milton's hunting and running a snare line, the other survival teams became upset that Milton, being the youngest and lowest ranking survival student, wasn't required to cut fire wood or cook for his team.

Squadron Leader Murray quickly told the complainers to mind their own business because his team was well satisfied with Milton's contribution to the team effort. The instructors also sided with SL Murray and Milton. The instructors reminded the complaining teams that they had the same options as Milton's team to use the team member considered most qualified to hunt food. Complaining didn't fill a hungry stomach, but hunting would.

No one from the other teams managed to catch a rabbit or shoot a grouse during the entire time spent at the bush survival camp. None of them made much effort and consistently complained about being hungry and cold. Sure, Milton was experienced at snaring wild game, but any member of the other teams could have at least worked hard at procuring game to supplement their issued rations. Placing several snares in strategic locations along rabbit trails would produce a rabbit eventually. Each day he had to venture further from camp to find wild game. There were only a limited number of rabbits and grouse in one small area.

Milton's camp decided, since the temperature continued to hover fifty below or colder each night, to take some of the rocks from their fire bed and after heating wrap each in parachute cloth and place in and at the foot of the sleeping bags. It was a real pleasure to retire at night in the preheated sleeping bags.

Again, the suggestion came from Squadron Officer Murray.

Some days Milton would roam several miles in quest of game and for the excitement of seeing new areas. The snow was about four feet deep, necessitating travel by snowshoes. He kept extending the snare line and following the tracks previously made by his own snow shoes. It was easier walking in his old tracks and he would set snares in rabbit trails crossing his snowshoe trail.

Once a moose crossed his trail and he was tempted to try killing it with the .22 caliber, single shot rifle. He aimed at the moose, but hesitated because the moose was large and very intimidating, especially to a person armed only with a .22 caliber single shot rifle. Climbing a tree to escape a wounded and angry moose while wearing snowshoes was an impossible task. Luckily, common sense prevailed and Milton stood and watched the majestic moose walk deeper into the dark Spruce trees. The moose was truly a king of the forest.

Milton, being young and somewhat a dreamer, thought of the impression he would have made in camp if he had downed the moose with his .22, and they would have had all that delicious meat to eat. He wondered how long it would have taken then to consume the entire moose.

Back in camp, he related to the instructors how he had seen the moose and had been tempted to shoot it with his small caliber rifle. He was told that it was good that he hadn't shot at the moose and only wounded it. Moose could be very dangerous when wounded. Besides the Canadian Fish and Game authorities wouldn't have liked the idea of an American killing a moose, especially out of season.

One of the instructors explained to Milton that in an actual survival situation, the survivor should be alert to shoot any type of wild game that could be located. He explained to Milton the vital areas on a moose's body that could be hit with a small caliber rifle with any expectation of a kill.

Milton thoroughly enjoyed the survival training at the camp near Fort Nelson, BC and especially the opportunity to hunt each day for food for his camp. The members of his team would always greet his return from a hunting trip with enthusiasm because most days he would have something for the stew pot. One trip he discovered another survival camp unknown to his camp.

That camp consisted of members of the Strategic Air Command, who were testing aircraft equipment such as radios, survival rifles and clothing. They had plenty of food and offered Milton extra rations. He refused to accept the extra ration, but did take some dehydrated onions, salt and pepper to flavor the evening stew. These items were an instant hit with his team. The evening stew was better than ever. The other team members and instructors, too, wondered how the stews were so flavorful and smelled so wonderful.

For three days the temperature dropped to about sixty degrees below zero at night. It was so cold that smoke from the campfires would only rise to tree top level. During the night trees could be heard popping as a limb froze and fell to the ground. Milton poured himself a cup of steaming hot tea and sat it behind him to cool only to discover that a rim of ice had formed in less than five minutes. That was cold! Yet they slept warm because of their sleeping arrangements.

The day before the team was scheduled to leave the survival camp, Milton was summoned to the instructor's tent and invited to sit in a real chair and have a cup of tea with them. The inside of the tent was like being inside a house. It was warm and cozy. The head instructor – Warrant Officer Goody – wanted to talk to him.

WO Goody told Milton that he was pleased with his progress in the survival training. He told Milton stories about his pre-military employment as a Royal Canadian Mounted Policeman in the Arctic and about some of his experiences in that job. He related a story about the "Mad Trapper of Rat River." That true story was about a man arriving in the North Country in the 1930s and started trapping in the wilds of the Northwest Territories.

Some one resented his presence and started stealing animals from his traps. The man discovered the thief and in the argument that followed, shot and killed the man. The killing was actually self-defense. He should have reported to the RCMP and have let them handle the incident. For some reason he wanted nothing to do with the police since he had taken the law into his own hands.

A member of the dead man's family informed the RCMP of the incident and two policemen snowshoed to his cabin to arrest him. The man resisted arrest and evaded the police. He proved to be an expert outdoorsman and for a time ran circles around the RCMP. The chase covered a large area of the North Country.

WO Goody had been one of the RCMP in on the chase from start to finish. The man would reverse his snowshoes to confuse those tracking him. Time after time he was trapped only to shoot his way out and in the process killed two more men who had been chasing him. The RCMP developed a respect for the man's ability and after finally cornering him in a cabin, gave him the opportunity to toss his gun out and surrender. His answer was more gunshots. The man probably thought that he had nothing to lose and refused to surrender.

After the cabin had been silent for several hours without a shot fired, Officer Goody and several other policemen cautiously approached the cabin and peering through cracks between the logs discovered the fugitive dead. He had been shot and between his teeth was a partially devoured raw ground squirrel.

They felt sorry for the man who they had chased for those several months and the fact that he had lost his life. He had presented the RCMP with a challenge like never before. No one was able to discover the true identity of the man. He had given his name as Johnson at the Trading Post when purchasing supplies when he had first arrived in that area. The fugitive's efforts at evading capture created a certain amount of respect from those chasing him.

He had on his body a money belt containing several thousand US dollars, he spoke with an American accent, and at his death had no identification on his body. Milton was thrilled to hear that and other stories from the instructors. Listening to the men telling their stories made Milton feel like he had taken part in the chase and the other adventures.

Warrant Officer Goody told Milton that one of the reasons he had been sent for was to congratulate him on how well he was doing in the Survival School. Because of his performance, he was excused from additional woodland survival training. He was asked if he would like to spend the next day with a professional hunting guide and help the man search for several pack horses that had strayed from his hunting camp before the heavy snows had come. The horses were somewhere in that part of the wilderness area.

Milton was more than glad to accompany the guide in the search for his horses. Since he would be away from the camp the entire next day, he was issued two survival rations – one for him and one for the guide. Milton and the guide – his name was Joe – left the camp at first light the next morning and walked the entire day searching for the lost horses and only returned when forced to by darkness. They had found old horse tracks and lots of fresh moose tracks, but not the horses. Joe pointed out to Milton several types of scrubs and a grass growing next to trees called Beaver Grass. This grass was green all winter and was round like a small pencil. This was the food that kept the horses alive in the winter and moose, too.

One humorous incident occurred when Milton and Joe stopped for lunch. They cut a large pile of Spruce boughs and packed them atop the snow for a fire-base. Otherwise the fire would be extinguished from the snow collapsing under the hot ashes. They built a small fire and boiled tea water in the small pot that Milton carried in his pack. He warmed his can of meat by placing it in the tea water.

Joe placed his in the hot ashes and coals from the fire. Milton attempted to warn him about the danger of heating a can of meat in hot coals. Joe wouldn't listen and when the meat started to cook and expand in the can it exploded and threw hot juices and meat particles over both him and Milton. Milton shared his warmed can of meat with Joe.

The man said he had never tried warming a can of meat on an open fire before and was really surprised when it exploded. Milton only smiled and didn't bother to tell Joe that the same thing had happened to him when warming a sealed can over a camp fire in Alabama several years before. One incident was sufficient for Milton.

The warm camp and enjoying the evening stew was a wonderful experience after walking all day on snowshoes through the deep snow. While he had been away from camp an interesting event had occurred. Since it happened under a controlled situation, the event didn't create much of a problem. It was an eye opener when they discovered that the special Arctic Survival clothing they were testing would melt when it was too close to an open flame. One of the team had backed up to the campfire to warm himself and when he happened to glance down, he discovered that the entire rear of his special boot had melted and left his socks intact. The suits were condemned based upon that incident. The boot was wrapped in parachute cloth to keep out the snow.

The other two teams continued to grumble about Milton spending all his time hunting and the fact that he had failed to share the game he had taken with their groups. Yet, none of the other teams attempted to brave the extreme cold weather and hunt or set snares for rabbits. Actually, the wild game was shared with whoever happened to come over to their camp after they had eaten their evening meal.

Milton would have gladly taken anyone hunting with him if they had asked. Squadron Leader Murray and the instructors again told the other groups what they thought of the little effort they had exerted in applying survival skills learned in the class room to actual survival conditions such as they were undergoing at the present time. The sentiments voiced by the instructors quieted those who were complaining and they never said anything more.

The hike back to the pick up point on the Alcan Highway went fast for Milton's team, but the other two teams were exhausted from lack of sleep and they had a difficult time walking the six miles with all their survival gear, and, on snowshoes. They plodded along and were thirty minutes behind the first team. All teams had started at the same time. At Fort Nelson, they were informed that a plane would pick them up at noon the next day for the flight to Yellow Knife, Northwest Territory and there they would spend the night before proceeding to Victoria Island north of the Canadian landmass in the Arctic Ocean.

The first thing all the teams did after arriving at Fort Nelson was visit a local restaurant and each person ordered three breakfasts consisting of ham, eggs, potatoes and toast, washed down by cup after cup of hot coffee. Each meal only cost seventy- five cents and the food was delicious. The waitress asked one of the students why everyone was so hungry. She stated that every time a class would return from the survival camp they would stuff themselves like they hadn't seen food in years. One of the team replied that they had been starved half to death for an entire week and now they were trying to make up for the missing meals.

While they had been at the survival camp, the temperature had dropped to between fifty and sixty below zero each night for five of the seven nights spent there. They were lucky there had been no wind because a strong wind would have made life miserable. Everyone was in a much better mood after such a big breakfast. The other team members became friendly with Milton once more. For a time they had made him feel like a leper.

After leaving the restaurant, Milton's team watched a hockey game. The Canadians were a hardy group and seemed to enjoy hockey-and later that evening played the Scottish game of Curling. Curling consisted of sliding a forty pound stone across the ice, a game similar to shuffle board where the objective is to slide a puck to a marked area. The game was a lot of fun and the team met many friendly Canadians.

The other two teams were very tired and had elected to return to the barracks immediately after leaving the restaurant to catch up on their sleep. They slept for the next fifteen hours. The purpose of relating how tired the other teams were is to reinforce the fact that under survival conditions it is very important to sleep and rest in order to maintain strength. Thanks to Squadron Officer Murray's recommendations, Milton's team received a good night's rest each night despite the severe cold.

Yellow Knife, Northwest Territories was a very interesting place to visit. That city reminded a person of an old western town with the many false front buildings. Yellow Knife was different because mixed with the old buildings were new modern buildings. There were gold mines within the city limits and lakes abounded where small planes could be seen landing and taking off on skis.

During the flight to Yellow Knife the plane flew over the Great Slave Lake and it was interesting to see a highway had been plowed through the snow on the ice and trucks and buses could be seen moving on the ice like on a main paved highway.

The teams visited a restaurant for their evening meal and a man introduced himself – Milton can't remember his name – but he was originally from Alabama. He had moved to Yellow Knife during the Great Depression and found gold. He owned a producing gold mine on the outskirts of town. He heard the students talking and recognized from their accents that some were Americans. He recognized Milton's accent as being from his own home area.

He just wanted to talk, and that he did. He treated everyone to a steak dinner and followed by drinks at the bar for those desiring to drink. Milton was only eighteen and didn't drink. Besides, the bartender wouldn't serve him because he was under twenty-one. Matter-of-fact, he was the youngest person in the Survival School. The next youngest person was twenty-three.

The team remained overnight in Yellow Knife and early the next morning, Milton and his team were told that they, and fifty small Spruce poles, would fly to Victoria Island in an old DC-3 and be off-loaded and the plane would return for the other two teams. The plane would land on the eight-foot thick ice in the fjord located next to the few buildings at Cambridge Bay.

The flight to Cambridge Bay was the most exciting event in Milton's young life. It was hard to believe that he was flying over parts of the Arctic that he had read about in books, never believing that he would ever have the opportunity to actually see that area. The Spruce trees at Yellow Knife had been no larger than 4 inches at their base and were 30 feet tall. In that area, trees grow slowly and the further north one travels, the smaller they become until a point is reached where no trees grow at all. This is known as the tree line.

Milton was impressed by the thousands of frozen lakes stretching as far as he could see from flying at eight thousand feet. Soon there was little snow as they flew further north. The land became rocky with huge boulders larger than houses sitting alone on rock formations. The scenery was awesome! Soon they neared the rocky, ice-filled coastal area of the strait separating the Canadian mainland from Victoria Island. What had once been only a few lines and notations on a map had become reality before Milton's eyes.

The closer to Victoria Island they came, the more clouds were building up. Soon the ground was obscured from the air. When the DC-3 reached Victoria Island, the clouds were down to three hundred feet and dropping. The pilot circled the landing area three times, and because there was a five hundred foot radio tower, which was definitely a hazard in that weather, he decided to return to Yellow Knife and try the flight again the next day. Everyone gave a sigh of relief because landing beside a metal tower projecting unseen into the clouds was too much of a risk to take.

The DC-3 landed at the airport in Yellow Knife ahead of the storm that had closed Cambridge Bay. It snowed most of the night and by early dawn, the sky was crystal clear and calm.

The pilot loaded half of the survival students aboard, including Milton's team, and arrived at Cambridge Bay without incident. The radio tower was sticking up in the air along side the section of eight-foot thick green ice that was used as a runway. Landing on ice was a new experience for Milton. The landing was smooth and after taking what seemed forever to stop, the plane turned and taxied back to where several long low buildings were located. There was a Royal Canadian Mounted

Police Office and living quarters, a barracks for the ten Canadian Air Force men stationed there, and a Hudson Bay Company Trading Post.

On the far side of the inlet where they had landed was an Eskimo village consisting of small shacks constructed from packing crates, animal skins, and snow blocks. Adjacent to each Eskimo house several dogs were tied to stakes. The dogs were huge and savage appearing. They were tied apart to prevent fights.

The team spent the night in one of the low barracks and the plane returned to Yellow Knife to bring the rest of the survival students to Cambridge Bay so the barren land survival training could begin. Surviving in the high Arctic was more difficult than in the bush land. The importance of having the right equipment and clothing was emphasized.

The next morning the instructors assembled everyone and loaded the sleeping bags and other equipment on a large sled pulled by a caterpillar driven by the smallest Eskimo that Milton had ever seen. All the Eskimos that Milton observed on Victoria Island were about five feet or shorter. He could hold his arms out and the Eskimos could stand upright and walk under them.

The Eskimo driving the caterpillar told the instructor that a storm was coming and that he didn't want to drive the several miles to the lake where the team was to practice survival. The instructor told him, "No storm, I've checked with the weather man."

But the Eskimo repeated, "Storm coming." And he refused to drive any further with the caterpillar-drawn sled. The instructor insisted and so the Eskimo deliberately drove the caterpillar into a deep snow bank.

The instructor grew angry with the Eskimo who got down from the caterpillar and started walking with angry, long strides back to his house across the bay. The instructor walked back to the barracks and returned with two other Eskimos and another caterpillar. They freed the stuck machine and the team followed along behind the caterpillar-drawn sled about five or six miles to a large freshwater lake.

At the frozen lake, two Eskimos were pulling a fishnet through a hole in the eight-foot thick ice. The fish were removed and then the holes would be covered with thick snow blocks to keep the hole from freezing. Milton had never realized how ingenious the Eskimos were. The men were using long ropes to pull the net in and out from under the ice. The net contained forty or fifty large Arctic Char, similar to trout.

Squadron Office Murray asked for and received two of the three feet long Char. The day was spent building igloos and other types of shelters in the thirty-below-zero weather. Main emphasis was placed on digging in to be out of the wind. The wind consistently blew from the northwest. With a combination of low temperature and wind, freezing was an ever present danger. Survival students gave the appearance of being vain because occasionally each student would pull out a signal mirror and check their face for signs of frozen spots. Such spots will appear yellowish white and feel stiff.

Late in the afternoon, which is about one p.m. (the days are short in that part of the Arctic in February) the wind started blowing harder and the temperature continued to drop. Early in the day, the temperature had been thirty below, and Milton would later discover that the night's temperature had dropped to fifty-seven below with a forty-five mile per hour wind.

The reluctant Eskimo had been correct in insisting that a storm was coming. The Canadian weathermen were surprised by the unexpected storm. With all of their modern scientific weather equipment they were caught completely by surprise when the storm blew in. Milton wondered how the Eskimo knew that a storm was coming and the trained weathermen with their instruments didn't. That was one of the mysteries of the Arctic and its native people.

The instructors and the Eskimos were in a hurry to get the students back to the warmth of the barracks and out of harm's way. So Murray walked over to Milton and asked if they were going to let a little cold weather and storm beat them. "Definitely not," responded Milton. So Murray asked if any other members of the team would like to spend the night in the freshly built igloo with him and Milton. There were no volunteers.

Murray and Milton crawled into the igloo with their equipment and sealed the three-foot entrance with their packs and snow blocks. One of the Eskimos had loaned them a caribou skin to place on the sleeping platform under their sleeping bags. A candle was used for heat and light. The wind howled all night, but they were snug inside the igloo. The temperature inside the igloo was 32 degrees above according to their thermometer. Two candles were the only heat used most of the time in the igloo, except when heating water on the small alcohol burning stove used for cooking. Because of fumes and a shortage of fuel it was impractical to use the stove for heat.

The Arctic char had frozen solid immediately when exposed to the below zero weather. With a hatchet, they chopped one of the fish into hunks and boiled it on the small stove that they used only for cooking and heating water. The temperature stayed low and the wind blew all the next day, but Murray and Milton were comfortable. They played cards by candlelight.

After the big storm blew itself out, Murray and Milton ventured from their snug igloo and were treated to a view of buttermilk skies and new drifts of fresh snow blown in from the northwest. In that particular part of the Arctic, there is little snow compared to a northern state like Maine. But what snowfall there is, is dry and blown constantly by the wind and piled against hillsides creating deep drifts.

Snow has to be a certain consistency to be used for making snow shelters such as igloos. They discovered that without an Eskimo to direct their efforts and actually assist with the construction, an igloo was very hard to make. It took Milton and Murray the best half of a day to make an igloo that would have taken an Eskimo not more than an hour.

To select the proper snowdrift, a large butcher knife was pushed through the snow to test its consistency. When a properly packed snow drift is located, blocks measuring 36"x18"x12" were cut from the drift and the blocks positioned in a spiral arrangement. Snow was stuffed in the cracks to block airflow.

After an igloo had been used overnight, it would be strong enough to stand on. Fresh constructed igloos are well insulated by the snow blocks. Matter of fact, the Eskimos told the instructor that polar bears had actually climbed over their igloos sniffing their odor and clawing at the snow blocks to get to them. The bears most likely envisioning a free meal out of the inhabitants! Often their sled dogs would worry the bear until it forgot about the meal inside and shuffled off to find an easier prey. If the dogs failed to drive the bear away, the bear would have to be shot.

Before the white man arrived and provided them with modern weapons, the Eskimos would spear polar bears. It was a test of bravery to walk up to the huge white bear and stab it with an ivory-tipped spear when it stood up on its hind legs to grab them. The objective was to drive the spear as deeply into the bear's chest as one could. Most of the Eskimo were short in stature, but had barrel chests and tremendous strength.

Milton and Murray had a 30.06 rifle along in the event a polar bear decided to try and make a meal out of them. They aspired to shoot a polar bear for its splendid fur coat. The polar bears in remote areas have no fear of men because they are so seldom in contact with humans. For this reason, the bears tend to be dangerous opponents. Every creature is considered a potential meal by the polar bear.

Late in the afternoon after Murray and Milton had dined on more of the Arctic Char the Eskimos had given them – even eating some of it raw by shaving frozen bites from the fish – the rest of the teams came out and the training proceeded. Different types of shelters were constructed, using the little talent possessed by the students.

The easiest shelter to construct from snow was a trench, using the blocks of snow cut from the trench for a roof. The main concern in the high

Arctic regions is to get into shelter from the prevailing wind. A trench served that purpose.

Thanks to the special nylon suits the survival students were testing, they stayed warm. Even at 57 degrees below zero the suits remained comfortable. The hood of the one-piece suits extended over six inches in front of the face and wire was built into the face portion of the hood so that it could be shaped as desired to keep the wind out.

As mentioned before, those wonderful suits never accepted as regular issue because of the danger from fire causing them to melt. Imagine attempting to escape from a flaming aircraft wearing one of those suits.

When it was time to return to the barracks and await the C-47 to return for them Milton, Murray and the rest of their team decided to walk back instead of riding the caterpillar drawn sled. The caterpillar trail ran about six miles and was easy to follow.

Almost no vegetation could be seen except on the side of the hills and areas kept clear of snow by the prevailing northwest wind. In some areas a few Dwarf Willows bushes could be seen sticking up above the snow. And of course, there was Caribou Moss on most of the rocks.

The walk back was very interesting even with the wind blowing with gusts up to forty miles per hour and the temperature still hovering at minus forty degrees below zero. Fortunately, the wind was blowing from the side instead of head on. It was easy to adjust the hoods on the survival suits to prevent wind from entering and freezing faces. Exposure to that icy wind would result in an immediate frostbite and severe freezing of the face with any prolonged exposure. Milton had experienced several spots of frozen tissue on his face while on a dog team trip in Labrador.

On Victoria Island, as with other areas of the Arctic, the ground is frozen with permafrost the year round and only thaws a few inches in the summer. Burying the deceased on Victoria Island wasn't a simple matter. Most of the time crude coffins were made from packing crates or else the body was wrapped in caribou skins and placed on hills and covered with rocks to keep fox, wolves and hopefully, polar bears from digging up the body and enjoying a feast. In that and other harsh climates everything is a meal for animals including mice and lemming.

The hike back to the barracks was very educational in that one could appreciate trekking across Arctic terrain. The prevailing wind had packed the snow so hard that snowshoes weren't needed. The snow was so dry that each step produced a grinding sound because of the extremely dry snow. The Eskimos apply a thin layer of mud and fresh water mixture over the steel runner of their dog-pulled sleds, because the steel runner wouldn't slide across the dry snow caused by excessively low temperatures.

Milton observed the largest flock of grouse that he had ever before observed. These birds are tasty and are the size of a Cornish game hen. Normally, back at Goose Bay, the flocks consisted of six to twelve birds. The flock seen by Milton must have numbered several hundred. Milton wished he had a shotgun with him instead of the 30.06 caliber rifle. Also during the hike back to the barracks the teams spotted wolves, polar bear and fox tracks, but no animals. The loud noise they made walking on the dry snow must have scared all the animals away. The Eskimo with their skin boots hardly made any noise when they walked. Once back to the barracks he and Murray found the interior almost too hot for comfort after sleeping in an igloo. Admittedly, the mattress felt wonderful and Milton had no problem sleeping that night.

While waiting for the plane to arrive and return them to Yellow Knife, they observed an antique plane landing on the ice and everyone rushed down to the landing area to get a closer look. The strange and very old plane was a 1928 Ford three motor plane constructed from corrugated metal.

A Canadian pilot had a contract to haul supplies to Hudson Bay Company Trading Posts in various areas of the Arctic with that old, but dependable plane. Like the C-47, the Ford Tri-motor was on skis to facilitate ice and snow landings. The skis weren't that good because of the dry snow found in that part of the Arctic, but they were ideal for landing on ice. Bays and rivers became a natural runway in the winter and by February the ice would be about eight feet thick and very safe for landing.

The old plane was leaking oil from two of its motors and the crew chief was wiping oil from the cowling and pouring more oil into the motor's reservoirs from five-gallon cans. He remarked that "oil was cheaper than motor overhauls." The survival students assisted in rolling two barrels of gasoline to the plane from a supply covered with a canvas on the shore of the Bay.

The fuel was hand pumped into the plane's fuel tanks. The entire scene reminded Milton of how things must have been during the early days of aviation. The survival students, some who were jet fighter pilots, found humor in the event surrounding the old plane that flew at about eighty-five miles per hour while their jets flew four to five hundred miles per hour. They were almost in awe of flying in such an "old crate," as they called the Ford Tri- motor.

Later in the afternoon, just before dark, the DC-3 arrived and flew the team back to Yellow Knife. The clean, warm hotel room, and the delicious food found in the hotel restaurant was hard to beat when compared to that found at Cambridge Bay. Outdoor living is nice, but the comfort of a warm hotel room and shower were hard to beat. The only problem was that the hotel room was almost too hot after sleeping out in the cold.

After a debriefing in Edmonton and a test on all that was covered in the classroom, bush, and polar survival classes, Squadron Leader Murray of the Royal Canadian Air Force and Corporal Milton of the United States Air Force received honors as the Outstanding Graduates of the class. They were awarded the title of "Hikko Gnuk"-in Eskimo, meaning mighty man of the ice. They were both proud of that award.

Milton finally felt qualified to return to Goose Bay, Labrador and start the Survival School in operation again. The Canadian Survival School, along with all the books that Milton had read all his life about the Arctic proved beneficial and amply qualified him for teaching others how to survive in the Arctic and sub-Arctic regions.

Squadron Leader Murray told Milton that any time he wanted to leave the American Air Force, he would have a place for him in the Canadian Air Force teaching survival. Milton felt honored by SL Murray's offering him a position. In return, Milton thought that his success in the Survival Sschool was because of the effort put forth by that outstanding Canadian Officer. He gave Milton his address, but Milton never contacted him.

—10—

The Special Assignment

On June 26, 1950 when the Korean War started things changed drastically for Milton. One day a few months after the start of the war he was ordered to report to the Provost Marshal's Office located in Base Headquarters. Milton spent some anxious moments wondering what type of trouble he was in that would require reporting to the big boss. He had once given the Base Commander's wife a ticket because of an incident when he was on patrol. Surely, his summons to the Provost Marshal's Office couldn't be about that incident. The Provost Marshal was responsible for law enforcement and security for the Base.

When he was finally ushered into the Provost Marshal's Office, he was surprised to see the Base Commander with the Provost Marshal. Milton thought, as he saluted and stood at attention before the officers, that he must be in worse trouble than he could have envisioned. Sitting before him were the two top-ranking men assigned to Goose Bay. Perhaps the Base Commander was sore about his wife being written up by Milton? Milton wondered if his military career was over after serving in the Air Force for less than two years.

The Provost Marshal told Milton to be "at ease" and take a seat in a chair located next to where they sat. He was offered a cup of coffee that he politely declined. The men spent thirty minutes asking questions about the outdoors and his police duties. He was asked about his knowledge of the areas surrounding the base. Colonel Williams, the Base Commander, had seen him several times in the woodland near the Base. The Colonel enjoyed taking a walk in the woods near the base on a Sunday afternoon. He had seen Milton in the woods during one of his walks and had talked to him for a time.

The recent shooting incident in which Milton was involved was discussed in detail. The Base Commander told Milton that perhaps the shooting incident could have been handled differently, ... maybe avoided. That event had triggered an international incident between Canada and the United States because two Canadian citizens were involved. Milton nodded his head in agreement. The incident had been a nightmare for him and he was glad everything was over with. He didn't like to look back on that incident.

"However, had I been in your shoes, I might have done the same as you did," the Commander stated. Milton felt better after the Commander expressed this opinion. He had attended hearings in Newfoundland because of that incident. Finally, after discussing the Korean War and what was becoming known as the Cold War, Milton was asked his age. He replied that he was eighteen. The officers glanced at each other. The Commander said that he hadn't realized that Milton was so young. They told him to wait in the outer office until called back because they wanted to discuss something.

Twenty minutes later he was summoned back into the Provost Marshal's Office. After he was seated, the Base Commander asked Milton if he would like to work directly for him and the Provost Marshal. He told Milton that he had a special assignment for him and both he and the Provost Marshal felt he was well qualified for the job being offered. He didn't have to accept the assignment, it was strictly a volunteer assignment. Milton had always been told by older, more experienced servicemen to never volunteer for anything in the military.

Milton told the Commander that he was willing to work wherever the Colonel wanted him. (He knew that Colonels didn't have to ask someone to volunteer, they normally just volunteered a person for the job they wanted that person to do.) The Commander informed Milton that he was to be an Air Force Scout, and he would be one of only five or six scouts in the entire Air Force. He was to patrol the woodlands around the base. They felt that he had the qualifications needed for such a job. He was told that he could select an assistant from the Air

Police Squadron.

Milton felt elated to have been selected for that position. He would be given a special identification card signed by the Base Commander authorizing him access to all areas of the Base that he needed to enter to perform his duties as well as access to "Happy Valley." "Happy Valley" was an off-limits area that required special permission for a member of the Air Force to enter.

Milton's new duties would consist partly of controlling and recovering government property from the many cabins and dugouts hidden in the woodland around the Base. Most of these cabins and dugouts had been constructed by servicemen during World War II and by some of the natives.

A few of the cabins were being used for large scale gambling. There were several men on Base who were reputed to be professional gamblers who entered the service shortly after World War II for the express purpose of fleecing the Air Force personnel stationed at Goose Bay or anywhere else they might be stationed. Milton received information from a good source that in one year the two men had won over eighty thousand dollars, and that was a large sum in those days.

Many parties were held in those dugouts and cabins that resulted in the participants becoming staggeringly drunk. The danger of becoming drunk in the winter and dying from exposure from the extreme cold was a real possibility. Several people had already been severely frost bitten.

He was to frequently check the Happy Valley settlement, which was off-limits to military personnel, and arrest any Air Force personnel found there illegally. Also, he was to make friends with as many of the natives as possible. He was to identify the thieves and stop the stealing of government property perpetrated by a few of the natives from "Happy Valley." Most were honest, but there were a few that required watching. Some even openly bragged about stealing fuel oil from the Base so that they never had to cut firewood like most of the natives.

During the short summer when the ice melted from the bay, ships would arrive with a year's supply of food, materials and equipment for the Base. A small amount of government property turned up missing between the ships and the warehouse on the American side of the Base.

Supplies were hauled from ships by truck 24 hours a day during the shipping season. Apparently, some of the natives were tossing items off the trucks and into the brush and woods alongside the road to be retrieved at a later time. Milton was to attempt stopping that drainage of materials and supplies by apprehending the thieves and recovering government property.

Milton was to identify new arrivals entering Happy Valley and areas around the Base. There was a real danger of sabotage to Base facilities such as the fuel storage area and the Base's water supply. He was to apprehend anyone caught in the woods near the base that couldn't show a good reason for being there. And, he was to monitor off duty Air Force personnel who were camping and fishing on the river and lakes near the Base. Fortunately, only a few personnel ventured from the Base. Most remained on Base and grumbled about being assigned to an isolated base where in their words, "There was nothing to do."

The Commander informed Milton that he should wear native clothing. The skin boots and non-military appearing clothing would better fit his job. He was to report to the Provost Marshal once each week and never be absent over a few days without reporting in. He could call from guard posts. He was told to always go armed off base. He was issued a .45 caliber pistol, a .12 gauge shotgun and a parachutist .30 caliber M-2 carbine with a folding stock.

The Base Commander told Milton, "I think you are an accomplished outdoorsman and very mature for your age. You should try and exercise good judgment in all your dealings with the natives and military personnel." He told Milton that as be became eligible for promotion, he would be promoted ahead of others competing with him. That sounded good to Milton.

Milton felt proud of being offered such an unusual job. The hours would be long and difficult to maintain, but for a person who loved the outdoors it was like being in heaven. The scout position was a job that Milton thoroughly enjoyed the entire time spent at Goose Bay.

Milton was permanently assigned the cabin he was presently occupying to live in and to be used as headquarters from which to operate. It would be a place to maintain his dog team that had grown to six huskies. He was assigned an assistant who he had been allowed to select from several volunteers from the Air Police Squadron.

The assistant was to help maintain the dog team and be available to assist Milton wherever he was needed. The tour of duty at Goose was 12 months and each of Milton's three assistants rotated to the States as soon as their year was completed. He couldn't talk any of the men into extending their tour of duty. Each man told him he was crazy to keep extending six months at a time when he could be back in the States. Milton disagreed with their views because he was living a dream and getting paid too. He could hunt and fish to his heart's content, and be paid while he did so. Wow, what a life!

Milton was authorized by the Base Commander to draw supplies from the Commissary Warehouse. Milton and the many native visitors ate well while he was there. Many natives who stopped by the cabin tasted bananas for the first time in their lives, and for many, eggs. One native borrowed a Sears Catalog and thought he was ordering a woman for thirty-nine dollars. All he received through the mail was a woman's dress. He was very disappointed. He had thought that American women must be desperate for a husband and advertised in the Sears Catalog.

The first major project that Milton undertook was locating and inspecting all cabins and dugouts around the Base and determining who was using them. Once he learned the location, he raided all the cabins and dugouts, assisted by several Military Policemen temporary assigned to him, and a large four wheel drive vehicle. He collected six truckloads of government property. Some of the property dated back to World War II when the Base had been very active.

Milton knew who was using the cabins by then and for what purposes. He made no effort to arrest these persons, instead he put them out of business by stripping the cabins of all government property. He collected oil heaters, barrels of fuel oil, cook stoves, bunks, blankets, sleeping bags, chairs and tables, record players and numerous other items of government property including canned food. The value of the equipment recovered was over thirty thousand dollars.

Milton wasn't too well liked by a certain segment of the Base population after that raid. Many threats were voiced against him. In time, most of the men realized that if Milton had made arrests they would have faced a court martial and possible dismissal from the service with a bad discharge. Some of them began to feel lucky at not being arrested and modified their feeling toward Milton. Thereafter, the cabins were consistently monitored and campers using them overnight never realized they were being spied on.

Milton attempted to resolve the problem with military personnel entering Happy Valley illegally. He would spend hours on the higher elevation above Happy Valley becoming familiar with where different people lived in that small village of four hundred souls. When someone new entered the area, they would live in a tent initially and later erect a tarpaper shack on the edge of Happy Valley.

Because of his relationship with several natives he was able to quickly discover information about anyone new entering Happy Valley. Whenever he would hear talk of military personnel visiting the girls in Happy Valley, he would attempt to apprehend them.

A cook from the Base Mess Hall was one of several people apprehended for entering Happy Valley illegally. This man had a nasty attitude and almost begged to be caught. He would brag to his co-workers about his girlfriend in Happy Valley and dared anyone to attempt catching him in that off-limit area.

He carried a large butcher knife when away from the Base and told several persons what he would do with that knife should Milton attempt to arrest him. Whenever Milton would occasionally eat in the Mess Hall, that man would always have a silly grin on his face when he served meals. Milton became determined to catch that man.

The one road to Happy Valley was a dirt-gravel road and was guarded by a checkpoint where a guard inspected all vehicles, sleds, or persons turning into the Happy Valley road. It was difficult for a person to enter illegally by that road. Milton wondered if there were other trails to Happy Valley, so he asked for a ride on the base's C-47 when the few pilots assigned to Goose Bay at that time did their monthly flying to qualify for flight pay.

All the plane did for about two hours was circle the Base at about a thousand feet so Milton had an unobstructed view of the road and trails into Happy Valley. From the air he discovered two trails unknown to him leading to Happy Valley. One was a half mile above the check point and the other trail was located past the guard shack about a mile down the road along side the river.

Milton spent two days monitoring the first trail and observed several natives pass. Some of the natives he knew, some were strangers. Apparently, they were never aware of his presence. No military personnel passed where Milton was hidden in the brush beside the trail. The next two days – one of those days when he knew the cook was off duty – he spent alongside the trail located near the river.

He positioned himself across from an island

where the trail crossed into Happy Valley. Anyone following that trail would have to wade across a thirty feet section of river that was only knee deep. The day was cold and rainy when Milton concealed himself in the Alder bushes that grew profusely along side the trail. He was dressed in a green poncho to keep dry and blended into the foliage.

Again, a number of natives passed his hiding place without observing him. During the second day of waiting in the Alder bushes, just before noon, he was about to give up on any military personnel entering the Valley from that trail. He was cold, tired and hungry.

As he started up from his place of concealment, he spotted a flash of red as someone came out of the woods onto the trail leading through the island. He hunkered back into the Alder bushes and observed the cook and a girl, walking arm in arm down to the water where they removed their shoes and socks and waded across the narrow stream. The girl was wearing a red coat. When they had waded across the stream, they stopped within twenty feet of Milton to put on their shoes and socks.

Milton quietly stepped out of the Alder bushes in front of the pair. They stopped in their tracks and appeared in a state of shock. The man had the infamous butcher knife in his belt, but when he recognized Milton, he said, "Don't shoot, here's my knife."

Milton hadn't drawn his .45 caliber pistol, but the man acted like he was being held at gunpoint.

"I'll go along peaceful and won't give you a hard time," he stated in a quivering voice.

Milton told him to take the knife from his belt and drop it on the ground. He hastily removed the knife with trembling hands and dropped it to the ground and pushed it toward Milton with his foot.

The girl was angry and finally anger gave way to tears. Milton told her she could leave and she hurried back across the stream without removing her shoes and socks. He escorted the cook to the Boat Club located about a half mile away and called for an Air Police Patrol to come and take the cook to the Base and jail.

The cook was court-martialed and received four months in prison and a bad conduct discharge from the Air Force. The Court was especially hard on him because of his bragging and the threats he had voiced to several people about what he would do to Milton. Word spread on the Base about his apprehension and military trial. That incident served as a deterrent to other personnel from entering the valley without the authorization from the Base Commander.

On occasions, members of the Base Chapel would make a special trip there on a Sunday morning for a joint church service. This visit was sanctioned by the Base Commander and written authorization given. Once a native who didn't like Milton reported him to the Provost Marshal for being in Happy Valley. He and the Provost Marshal had a good laugh about that report. He was told to be more careful in the future.

Discovering and keeping tabs on people who had somehow come to Goose Bay without authorization was a difficult task. Because of the friendship he had developed with several natives, they would alert him whenever someone new moved into the area from other parts of Labrador, Newfoundland or Canada.

The area was isolated and there were no roads to Goose Bay. The only way to get there was by air, a ship during a few months in the summer and by dog team in the winter. Many new arrivals came from the coast because they heard living was easier around the Base. His special relationship with several of the natives proved to be a valuable asset. They would always give him the latest news.

Milton would turn in anyone he discovered to be new arrivals in the area to the Royal Canadian Mounted Police for further investigation. He worked closely with Corporal Norris and Private Cheeseman on several cases. They were two very interesting people. They had the responsibility of patrolling a vast area and maintaining civilian law and order. Each spring, in April, one of them would travel to the coast and visit several villages by dog team. That patrol would require sometimes six weeks. That was before dependable motorized snow sleds were available. Dogs didn't break down like machines did at that time. When either policeman returned from a patrol, their faces would be tanned and burnt from the sun reflecting off the snow and ice. You didn't have to ask then if they had been on patrol. Their suntan said it all.

Time flew and Milton lived one exciting adventure after the other throughout each summer and winter.

—11—

Buck and the New Dog

Milton was introduced to a little, middle aged, bent over man in January 1951 by another native from Happy Valley. The man was no taller than four feet when he walked bent over with a stick in each hand for support. Milton felt sorry for him after he was introduced and seeing the plight of the man. After being so active all his life, Milton couldn't believe a person could live in that cold country where snow was on the ground at least nine months each year, and be so crippled as that man.

The man had heard of Milton and wanted to meet him. The native friend told Milton — like it was a joke — that the little crippled man wanted to work for Milton and be paid in room and board. The man claimed that he could cut wood, feed the sled dogs, clean the cabin, cook and watch after the cabin in Milton's absence.

Milton answered this request with a resounding "NO". But to be polite and not embarrass the little man, Milton talked to him for a time and was so impressed that he changed his mind and invited him to move into the cabin. Milton was away from the cabin often, and at that time didn't have an assistant, so the man would be useful as a caretaker.

The man's name was Buck and he proved to be a wonderful companion and he liked to talk and tell jokes. He knew almost everyone living in Happy Valley and told Milton many interesting things about many of the people living there.

After they became close friends, Milton learned something of Buck's early life. His parents had died from TB when he was young and he was sent to a Mission School in St. Anthony, Newfoundland. Buck had hated that place and the people in charge. He thought they looked down on native children from Labrador as being backward and somehow not as good as the local Newfoundland children. Whether that attitude existed or not, Buck had the impression that was the way things were.

Time after time, in the summers, he would run away from the Mission School only to be located and returned. He would always be severely punished for the trouble he caused by running away. His hatred for the school intensified until one night he poured a can of kerosene on the school building floor and set it afire and fled. The school was totally destroyed.

Buck was caught, but he was too young to be jailed so he was returned to the mission and closely controlled day and night. Soon afterward he was stricken with polio and as a result of that terrible disease, his body was crippled and for a long time he couldn't walk. Now he could only walk slowly with the aid of at least one walking stick. His walking sticks were cut from tree limbs and carved to form a knob to fit the palm of his hands.

Buck lived about a year with Milton and he appeared to enjoy the good food which Milton was supplied from the Base Commissary's Warehouse. They became good friends, too. He proved to be invaluable to Milton because of his knowledge of the inhabitants of Happy Valley. He told Milton which of the natives consistently stole from the Base. He might be crippled, but he was very intelligent and a good observer of people.

Through the efforts of a newly assigned and goodhearted Sergeant with connections to officials in the March of Dimes program in the States, Buck was provided two aluminum walking sticks. These canes fit the contour of his arms and made walking much easier. He was a grateful person because of the gift of the walking sticks and treasured them as his most valuable possessions. The goodhearted man was Sergeant Jordan who had visited Milton and had gotten to know Buck through those visits. Jordan loved the outdoors and would exchange stories with Buck for hours at a time.

Milton often wondered what quality of life a person in Buck's situation would enjoy. Buck was always pleasant to be around. He showed no self-pity for the lot life had dwelt him. He disliked returning Buck to Happy Valley, but his duties became more complicated and he was assigned an assistant from the Base.

Often, he would bring Buck to the cabin to spend a few days with him and his assistant. Besides, Buck would bring him up-to -date on events transpiring in Happy Valley. He learned of several new arrivals to Happy Valley through Buck. He turned the newly arrival names into the Canadian authorities for investigation.

Milton was always seeking additional sled dogs, especially since the area had just experienced a big die-off of dogs from Distemper, a disease that had spread among the dog teams.

His favorite dog Red had died from that animal disease. The Air Police Patrols, at Milton's request, would attempt to catch any stray dog that remotely looked like it could pull a sled and give it to Milton. That effort was some help, but the patrolmen captured few dogs. After all, who would want to attempt catching a large dog when not knowing its disposition. Looking at the large teeth of some of the sled dogs would discourage the bravest Air Policeman from attempting to grab such a dog. However, one dog was caught by a patrol and given to Milton.

That dog never became a decent sled dog and bit Milton several times when he attempted to hitch the creature to his sled. The other dogs in the team disliked that dog and were always attempting to take a bite out of its rear end. Milton finally turned the dog loose and allowed it to return to its original owner. That dog was most likely someone's pet and wasn't used to living outdoors in the cold.

Buck told him that Indians camped across the Hamilton River from the Boat Club had a dog for sale. The price of the dog was a fifth of whiskey. Milton knew that it was against the law to provide Indians with any type of alcohol whether by selling or donating. He wanted the Indian's dog very badly so he decided on another approach.

Milton purchased four cartons of Camel cigarettes from the Base Exchange for one dollar per carton. He planned to offer the cigarettes in trade for the dog. He was afraid some native would hear of the dog offered for trade and get there first. He hooked four dogs to his sled and traveled down the river and across the mile-wide river to the Indian encampment. They were camped across the river from what was once called the Boat Club.

There must have been twenty tents arranged in a large circle back from the riverbank in the shelter of thick Spruce trees. A bluish-white cloud of smoke from the many campfires hung low over the encampment. These Indians lived year round in tents. The tents were always white, well maybe gray would better describe them, and entire families lived in tents no larger than ten by twenty feet. They used a small stove in the tent in the winter for heat and cooking. In the summer they positioned the stove outside for cooking.

The tents were surprisingly warm in the winter. Milton had once been invited into an Indian tent in the winter when he was on the trail with his dogs. It was a very cold night and he was cold. He passed the camp of a family of Indians he knew and when they saw him, one of the Indians invited him in to get warm and drink a cup of tea.

He was surprised at the warmth of the tent and the hospitality of that Indian family. He wished they would have invited him to spend the night. That wasn't the case and he had to make a cold camp that night. He dug a hole in the snow and slept out under the stars. The Northern Lights gave an awesome and dazzling display of colors that night. It was a beautiful night and the stars appeared extra large. The temperature was twenty-five below zero. His double lined sleeping bag was warm so he had gotten a good night's sleep.

Most of the Indians would ignore white men. He remembered once when crossing Northwest River on bad ice. The Indians had lined the shore and cheered as he crossed that five- hundred feet section of rotten ice. The ice was breaking behind the sled and water was boiling up immediately behind the sled. And, yes, Milton was scared half to death with the thought of falling through the ice.

Milton thought he was a goner that time. Normally, most of the Indians were indifferent where white men were concerned. Perhaps they were cheering for the ice to break under the sled. Who knows?

Milton's presence when approaching the camp must have alerted every dog in the Indian encampment because they started howling and the small children ran for their tents as Milton walked down the trail from where he had tied his dogs on the river bank.

Soon several Indian men advanced to meet him near where the first tent was erected. They stared and Milton stared back for a long moment and finally one of the men asked what he wanted. The Indian spoke in broken English but appeared to understand English better than he spoke. Milton replied that he had heard of a sled dog offered for sale. He wanted to buy that dog.

The Indian turned and walked to the side of a tent and jerked a large black and white dog to its feet and it meekly followed its master to where Milton stood. The dog started growling at Milton, with the hair standing up on its neck and back. Its huge fangs looked menacing to Milton.

Milton backed slowly from the dog. As it leaped toward him, the Indian jerked on the rawhide rope holding the dog and proceeded to kick and beat it with a stick until it lay at his feet in submission. By that time Milton was reconsidering the thought of buying such an unfriendly dog. It appeared too ferocious. But, he felt sorry for the large dog because it was being beaten so badly by its master.

"How much do you want for the dog?" Milton asked. The Indian said one word, "Whiskey", and the rest of the Indians grunted in approval. "No whiskey" replied Milton. "The Canadian Police will arrest me and you, too, if I sell or give you whiskey." Milton told them.

Milton's statement caused the Indians to move a few paces away and huddle together. Milton could hear each Indian voicing his sentiments, at least that was what it sounded like because they were speaking in their own language with a few English words occasionally injected.

Finally the men returned to where Milton was standing and asked what he would give them for the dog. Milton pulled two cartons of Camels from inside his parka and offered those. All of the Indians grunted what sounded like disapproval. Then Milton pulled a third carton of cigarettes from his parka. The Indians again moved away a few paces and talked the deal over.

The Indian who spoke some English told Milton that he had a deal. To show his good faith, Milton gave them the fourth carton of cigarettes concealed in his parka. All the Indians grunted their approval of Milton's generosity. Milton had started to wonder why the Indians were selling the large dog.

He asked the Indian to harness the dog to his sled with an extra harness and trace he had brought along in the event his trade was successful.

To be honest, he was apprehensive about hitching the dog to the sled. It still looked like it would like nothing better than taking a bite out of him.

The first thing the new dog did was proceed to attack his four dogs. He was a snarling demon when it came to fighting. Milton waded into the midst of the fighting dogs attempting to separate them before one of his dogs was killed or severely injured. For his effort, the new dog bit him on the back of the hand. That was too much. Milton grabbed a snow-shoe from the sled and waded into the mass of fighting huskies and after a few well-placed blows proceeded to separate them. The Indians stood watching the entire episode with an amused look on their faces. It was his dog now and up to him to master the snarling creature. If animals can sense fear in a person, he must have known that Milton was somewhat scared of him.

When he undid the slip- knot on the rope securing the sled to a tree, the dogs made a mad dash down the trail to the frozen river and crossed the mile wide river at a fast pace. The new dog was used as a wheel dog. That meant he was the closest to the sled and couldn't reach the other dogs as long as they were moving ahead of him. And did they move!

The frustrated creature still managed to nip a few rear ends and that motivated the other dogs to a faster pace in an effort to escape the wild Indian dog. Rather than heading up river directly to his cabin, Milton decided to travel on the Base's frozen roads in a roundabout route that added about six miles to the trip back to the cabin. He wanted to run the dogs until they were too tired to fight, especially the new dog. He was worried about how he was going to unhitch the eighty-pound dog and attach him to a chain without being badly bitten.

The frozen Base roads were slick and the dogs had no problem pulling the sled at a fast clip, – Milton was once clocked by the Base Commander traveling through the small Base Housing area at twenty-two miles per hour. The speed limit there was fifteen miles per hour. The dogs covered the miles in record time.

While he was driving the team through Base Housing, he lost control when a Collie was leisurely strolling outside its owner's home. The entire team left the road and headed cross country after the Collie. The only thing that saved that dog was its speed and at the last moment, before the team could reach the Collie, Milton turned the sled over thereby making it difficult to pull through the deeper snow alongside the road.

The entire team, including the new dog, worked in harmony to reach the Collie. The Collie's owner – the Base Commander – saw what was happening and opened the door to his house and allowed the frightened Collie shelter. At Milton's next meeting with the Commander he was told that perhaps he should skirt the housing area in the future when he was traveling by dog team.

When Milton and his tired team reached the cabin – and he had ridden the sled in the deep snow instead of running behind the sled for the expressed purpose of tiring the team – he turned the sled over and tied it to a tree. The old team members were unhitched and chained in their regular places. When he approach the Indian dog, it backed away as far as the traces would allow, growling with fangs exposed and the hair standing up on the back of it's neck. Milton tried talking to the dog to calm it down.

Apparently the dog didn't understand English because it lunged at Milton and broke the skin on his hand with a slash from its long fangs. Milton jumped out of reach and grabbed a snowshoe and beat the dog until it stopped trying to attack him. Milton located a chain and collar and attached it around the neck of the growling dog. Some people have mentioned to Milton about how he beat his dogs. Those people should experience the same situation as Milton and perhaps they would change their minds.

He held a raised snowshoe in one hand in a threatening manner while attaching the chain with the other hand. He left the harness on the dog and untied the trace from the sled. When he fed the dogs their cooked cornmeal and grease containing several chopped up rabbits from the snare line, the new dog refused to eat. For a husky not to eat is almost unheard of, but that dog only growled and bared its fangs while ignoring the food. He left the food in front of the dog and the next morning most had been eaten and the remainder urinated on by the dog. That dog was being contemptible! Of course, he couldn't blame the dog for not liking cornmeal cooked with grease. That was all he had to offer and the other dogs never hesitated to eat all the food that he supplied.

The battle with the new dog continued throughout the balance of the winter with it being beaten several times and Milton's hands and arms bitten on numerous occasions. Fortunately, the dog slashed rather than seizing his arm. That dog's mouth was so powerful that it could crush a caribou's bone. Fortunately, none of the bites were very deep. Maybe the dog was just warning him to keep his distance.

The entire team appeared fearful of the Indian dog. When spring finally arrived and the ice had melted and flowed from the river – for three consecutive years the ice melted and started moving on the twenty-second of May – the dogs were tied under trees in the shade and apart from each other to prevent fights. They were quite capable of killing or seriously injuring each other. They seemed to enjoy fighting. Fighting was their form of entertainment judging from the constant flare-ups of temper exhibited by most of the dogs. Once when he had gone to the Hudson Bay store for a hundred pound bag of cornmeal to be used for dog feed, another new dog had irritated the rest of the team and they turned on him. The team slashed and ripped that poor dog until he was almost dead. There were few places on his entire body that didn't have a cut. The dog was incapacitated for three weeks and never got over its fear of the other dogs on the team. That dog had been notorious for starting fights and jumping out of the way and watching the other dogs fight. The team had somehow wised up to the trouble-maker and exacted their revenge. Dogs must be somewhat like humans.

Milton often had company at his cabin. On a number of occasions, in the early days, Colonel Williams, the Base Commander would visit Milton's cabin. He owned an old 1893 Winchester rifle that he always carried when he came down and practiced with it in front of the cabin. He informed Milton that as long as there was no drinking and partying at the cabin, Milton could live there. He wasn't going to allow the Scout Headquarters to become a party cabin like some of the other cabins that Milton had raided. He was really a nice gentleman and Milton had the greatest respect for him.

There were many visitors from the Base as well as natives from Happy Valley who would find an excuse to stop on their way to Muskrat Falls, some ten miles up stream. Milton would always have food for his guests. He learned to bake apple pie, yeast rolls, and make stews from rabbit, grouse, or porcupine. He didn't want to brag, but everything must have tasted good because his guests always cleaned up whatever he offered for a meal.

One Sunday, a Captain, the Commander of a Communication Squadron, his wife and two preteen daughters walked down to the cabin and told Milton that they had heard of him and the cabin and decided to come down, too. The man's wife had brought a freshly baked apple pie. After the first trip they would often come down on Sunday and have lunch with him. Milton enjoyed their company.

The Captain told Milton that he had served in the Navy during World War II as a PT Boat Commander. His stories were interesting and he and Milton became fast friends. Captain Fisher and his family seemed to enjoy the Sunday visits to the cabin. They would play checkers for hours at a time. Milton always looked forward to their visits.

The dogs were always jealous of each other and would fight at every opportunity. Milton usually watched the girls carefully so that they wouldn't wander too near the dogs and get mauled. The dogs would attack any creature unfortunately enough to be in reach of their chains. They were always attempting to kill the cat that Milton kept at the cabin to control the mice.

One day, Milton and the couple were seated at the large table drinking tea and playing cards when suddenly there was a tremendous commotion coming from where the dogs were chained. Milton noticed the girls weren't in the cabin. That scared him badly because he didn't know what fate would befall them should they stray too near one of the dogs.

He bounded out of the cabin and could hardly believe what he was seeing. The two little girls were playing with the Indian dog. One was on his back and the other was hugging him. Most unbelievable was to see that terrible dog licking the smallest girl's face.

After that incident, that dog became one of the best of Milton's team. He stopped attempting to attack Milton and became very obedient. The dog served faithfully for two years until he was lost on an eight day dog team trip across Lake Melville and into the Mealy Mountains. That's another story in itself.

—12—

The Cold War Heats Up

One evening in the summer of 1951, a series of events of a suspicious nature occurred. After dark, someone set an abandoned shack in Happy Valley on fire. The Canadian and American Base's fire trucks responded and attempted to control the fire before the woodlands were in flames. The moss was dry and waiting for a spark to set it ablaze.

While the fire trucks were busy in Happy Valley, a fire was reported in an empty barracks in the "G" area section on the far side of the American base. The remaining fire trucks were dispatched to fight that burning building and to prevent the fire spreading to the dry moss covered floor of the forest. Once all the fire trucks were fighting this second fire, the docks at Goose Bay below the Canadian side of the Base suddenly erupted in flames.

The dock fire was a more serious situation because ships hauling supplies had to dock there to unload. The docks were constructed from large Spruce logs and timbers. Before the fire engines could reload their trucks and respond to the new threat, the docks were burnt to water level.

The dock fire necessitated that all ships for the rest of the summer unload by lighter, (Lighters are smaller boats hauling supplies ashore from the ships anchored in the Bay). Using lighters required ten times as long to unload the ships. For the remainder of the shipping season there were always several ships anchored waiting their turn to be unloaded.

The docks were rebuilt from concrete, but only as winter approached, much too late to aid in that season's unloading of ships. The fire was thought to be sabotage, but by whom was the unanswered question. Milton turned all the information he had collected about the fire to the Office of Special Investigations.

Milton discovered that cans of gas and fuel oil had been positioned near where each of the three fires started. The timing of the fires couldn't have been by accident. Someone had ridden a motor bike from one site to another.

The Happy Valley and "G" area fires had been decoys to draw the fire departments away so that the dock fire would be so far advanced that there would be little hope of it being extinguished. Milton had discovered motor bike tracks and fuel cans at each site.

About three hundred yards from the dock area he located the motor bike and signs of a small boat having been pulled up on shore. No one ever claimed the bike and there were no identifying fingerprints on the bike. No one could remember ever seeing the small bike before it was discovered hidden in the brush near the water.

The person(s) responsible for burning the docks was never apprehended. Several days after the incident, a native living in a small village on the coast reported to the Royal Canadian Mounted Police that he had sighted a submarine on the surface of one of the inlets near his village. He had arrived just after daylight to check a net and to do some other work at that particular inlet when he sighted the submarine cruising out to sea.

The authorities confirmed that no American or Canadian submarines were operating in that area. There were many submarine sightings reported by natives living on the coast. Apparently, the submarines had something to do with the burning of the docks. Maybe some of the sightings were that of whales that frequented the coast of Labrador. Milton never discovered the answer to that puzzle.

The base's old C-47 made several trips to the coastal areas where the submarines had been sighted, but never discovered anything looking like a submarine. Lots of icebergs were sighted, but, no submarines. The flights were interesting and allowed the base pilots to do their training to help maintain proficiency and qualify for the small amount of flight pay they received each month.

Because of the fires, the Base remained on a state of alert for several weeks. The Provost

Marshal ordered Milton and his assistant to patrol the woods around the Base every day for a time. Emphasis was placed on protecting the Base's water supply that came from a small spring fed lake and the fuel storage tanks.

Those facilities already had guards posted and Milton roamed the woodlands around those areas without the guards realizing his presence. He was to apprehend anyone approaching those facilities through the deep woods. Milton felt like an Indian creeping silently through the woods. Now in old age Milton can hardly believe how quietly he once could walk through woodland.

If he found anyone "sneaking" through the woods anywhere near those facilities, he was to order them to halt and if they refused to obey his command, he was to shoot them. He went armed with the .30 caliber carbine set on automatic, and a .45 caliber pistol in a shoulder holster.

Once Milton did discover an Indian less than a hundred yards from the water supply and followed him, unseen, until he ascertained that the man was hunting and was no threat. He followed the Indian at a distance for a time and finally identified him as one who he had seen camping across the Hamilton River. This man and members of his tribe traveled to that area each year and camped at the same spot. Since the man and his family came down the river each summer to trade, he wasn't considered a threat.

Milton wondered what would have happened if he had challenged the Indian and the man had run away from Milton toward the water supply. That Indian couldn't speak English and Milton couldn't speak more than a few words of the Indian language. Would he have shot the Indian? Or would the Indian have attempted to shoot him? He wondered and was glad that he was not faced with having to make such a decision. He was prepared to shoot if the situation deteriorated.

During this time Milton patrolled the woods around the Base sixteen hours or more daily. When night would overtake him, he would stop and make camp, prepare food, washed down with many cups of tea boiled over a small fire, and sleep until about daylight and then patrol all day again. He would do this day after day. He had no problem sleeping at night.

The mosquitoes and gnats would often form a vast cloud around his head and even bite through his clothing. He generously used bottle after bottle of insect repellent in an effort to thwart the various insect attacks. The insects appeared motivated by the insect repellent to bite that much more. The insects were at their worse for a month after the snow melted each year.

It seemed to rain at least every other day during that summer. Often his meals would consist of roasted grouse or rabbit and boiled tea. Most of the time it was too much trouble carrying "C" rations.

Carrying his light sleeping bag, firearm, tea and a can for boiling water was more than enough to tote all day.

Initially, several natives stole items from the Base each night and took the stolen goods on the worker's truck to Happy Valley at midnight when the evening shift rode home. Milton would occasionally climb into the rear of the canvas covered truck bed before it departed the Motor Pool to pick up the native workers.

The driver wouldn't know that Milton was sitting in the rear of the truck. He wanted to make sure the native driver didn't tip off any would be thieves of his presence. There was a guard checkpoint at the entrance to the Happy Valley road, but the guards were very lax in carefully checking the workers for stolen goods.

One reason for the laxity in checking the truck was because it was usually packed with workers and to conduct a proper check required off-loading the truck and that was just too much work, especially in cold weather. None of the guards would do more than occasionally shine their flashlights into the mass of workers packed in the truck.

None of the guards ever recognized Milton sitting with the workers. He dressed like the natives and to the guards he was just another native headed home from working on the Base. Some of the guards thought that the natives looked alike with their skin boots, parka and other clothing.

When the truck arrived to pick up the native workers, Milton would be sitting in the darkened canvas-covered truck bed. The workers, in the dark, thought he was another worker. The first night that he did this, several men climbed on the truck with five-gallon cans of fuel oil or bags of items taken from their job sites. Apparently, taking things from the base was a normal and routine thing for some of the workers. However, it is fair to say that most of the men were honest and didn't steal. There is always a few rotten apples in every basket.

Just before the truck departed for Happy Valley some one lit a cigarette and in the flare of the match spotted Milton sitting quietly in the dark. When he was recognized, the persons having the stolen goods jumped out of the truck and deposited their loot by the door of the building in a neat line.

When they climbed back on the truck Milton never said a word, but shined his flashlight in each man's face so that he could recognize who they were. Sitting in the dark truck with all the natives made Milton hope that none of them were mean enough to stick a hunting knife into his side or back. In the darkness anything could happen.

After that incident most of the stealing stopped. If he would have arrested those he caught stealing, they would have been fired from their jobs and there were few jobs off Base. If they didn't work on the Base, the only option would have been to start living off the land once more and that was a harsh life after being accustomed to a pay check from the United States Government. One reason the stealing stopped was that the workers never knew when Milton would be on the truck, and they knew they wouldn't be given a break if they were caught stealing a second time. Maybe Milton was too soft hearted to see the men fired. He decided that there would be no second chance for anyone he caught stealing. One offense was all they were allowed.

Milton later became a friend of one of the men who he had caught stealing fuel oil. The man confessed that he had been heating his small shack several years with fuel oil taken from the base. He revealed that several men were taking fuel oil and no one at work had ever said anything about it, so he started taking oil. That habit had cost the Air Force many dollars. Milton's presence and the thought of getting caught had completely stopped the stealing of oil by that group.

When the Provost Marshal read Milton's report, he was, at first, upset because Milton hadn't arrested the men and made examples of them. Milton explained his reason for not arresting the men and the Provost Marshal listened patiently and heard Milton out and decided that perhaps the correct decision had been made. He informed Milton that there wouldn't be a second chance given to any native caught stealing. Milton had already made up his mind on that issue, too.

Because he hadn't arrested the men, they became friendly and kept him informed regarding events in Happy Valley such as new arrivals, unauthorized visits by Air Force Personnel, and tips on who was still stealing from the Base. Several of these men were of considerable help and made his job easier.

During the shipping season when material was being hauled from the docks to the American side of the Base, workers would toss items from the trucks as had already been mentioned. Milton recovered many different types of equipment and food that had been thrown from the trucks.

One day he discovered a new jeep motor still in its crate hidden beside the road in some brush. Many of the natives used jeep motors to power their fishing boats. That native and his friends had a surprise when they sneaked back the next night to retrieve the motor. As they picked up the crate to carry it further into the woods, Milton stood up from his place of concealment and the men lost their jobs after being escorted to the Canadian Royal Mounted Police Headquarters and booked for stealing U.S. Property.

Another item the natives liked was strawberry preserves. The preserves were shipped to the base in cartons of four, one gallon cans. Case after case was tossed off trucks to be recovered later. Many natives found their stolen strawberry preserves not too tasty because of the high cost of the stolen fruit.

No one ever gave Milton a hard time or attempted to resist arrest. His reputation had proceeded him. They all marched peaceful with Milton to the Royal Canadian Mounted Police Headquarters. He never had to point a gun or threaten any of those arrested. When several men were involved he exercised caution and was careful to have his weapon easily accessible...just in case.

The Base Commander was true to his word regarding promotions. Whenever Milton became eligible for promotion, he received a stripe. One promotion cycle when he was first eligible for Staff Sergeant, several personnel were more eligible than Milton for promotion. He was told to report to the Promotion Board – in Air Force Uniform – on a certain date. He seldom wore his uniform and had a difficult time finding a tie, so he borrowed a tie from one of his friends.

He had to wait to report to the board among several other men. Several of the other men waiting with him to meet the Promotion Board revealed that since they had more time in grade, they would be the ones to be promoted. Neither Milton nor the other five men knew that there was only one stripe available for Headquarters Squadron.

Milton said nothing. He was tired and still had to walk back to his cabin and feed the sled dogs. He only wanted to get the ordeal of dressing in his class A uniform, which included a tie, over with. Normally he wore native clothing and found wearing a tie very uncomfortable. Sure, he would like to be promoted, who wouldn't? Finally, he was called to report to the board.

The Promotion Board consisted of five officers. The entire time he was before the board, he was asked questions about the best fishing spots around Goose Bay and a few questions about his duties. He related some of the places he fished, and neglected to tell them that in the summer, he used a gill net to catch all the fish he needed to eat and food for his dogs. Fishing with a fly rod or rod and reel was too much work. All he had to do was set his gill net out late in the afternoon and take it up early the next morning and he would have an abundance of fish. However, he still was thrilled when he hooked a nice trout or large pike with his fishing tackle.

The chairman of the Promotion Board asked Milton if he would take him fishing one day. Milton agreed. When he was excused by the board and started out the door, the President of the Promotion Board gave Milton a wink and smile.

The following month when promotion orders were printed, Milton was the only man in the Headquarters Squadron to be promoted to Staff Sergeant. He was promoted from Private First Class to Staff Sergeant in less than twenty-six months. The extra pay came in handy. He spent little of his pay and saved most of it. After all, where in the woodland could he spend money?

**Buck, Milton and Sampon holding 11 rabbits
caught in Milton's snare line.**

Rev. and Mrs. Paul MacKinney with local children.

**Milton, 4th from left, with friends taking
boat trip to Northwest River.**

Bob, leader for Milton's dog team.

Fishing through the ice.

Rabbit snare set in trail.

**Rev. Dan MacKinney, returning from 10-day trip up
the Hamilton River. Fred Blake not shown.**

A Rescue Mission

Milton's First Month at Goose Bay

First Dog Team

New Hudson Bay Store at Goose Bay

The First Team

On Goose Bay

Plane Crashes on Ice of Goose Bay

The Scout

The Cabin

Two Members of the Semu Family

195

Mr. Semu

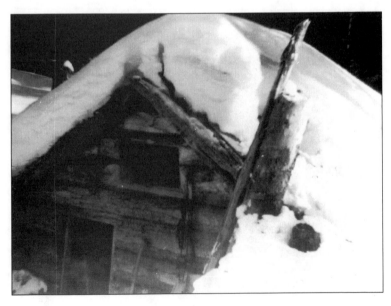

A Trapper's Cabin

A Native Trapper Having a "Boil-up"

L-R—Milton and Buck

Milton's Dog Team on the Hamition River

Nose Wheel Froze Causing Crash Landing   .

Canadian Survival Instructors

Milton in Front of Igloo at Cambridge Bay

199

Certificate Awarded by Canadian Survival School

B-45 Jet Bomber

Mountain Where B-45 Crashed

Rev. and Mrs. MacKinney with Danny

Frances and Milton

L to R, Danny, Beulah, Frances, Pastor and Mrs. MacKinney

Rev. Danny MacKinney

Cpl. Jones with Rabbit Caught in Snare

Hauling Supplies for Survival School

Paratepee Shelter Where Milton Lived for Three Months

Brush Shelter

The Survival Cabin—"Officers' Quarters"

Rev. Danny MacKinney with His Airplane

**Lt. Col. Douglas, Capt. Roy, Lt. Amidon, Capt. Matthews
Capt. Matthews Explaining the Principles of
Offset Intercept to Col. Douglas**

Milton Re-enlists for Another Three Years

—13—

The Norseman Rescue Mission

A Norseman high wing single engine airplane, piloted by a Canadian Air Force man, failed to return from a flight to Baffin Island. Once the plane was overdue and contact couldn't be established, the Rescue Squadron was alerted and a search was started.

Rescue planes flew a grid search in an effort to locate the plane and after three days of searching from dawn to dusk, the downed plane was discovered several miles off its planned flight path. The plane had crashed near a small lake and appeared from the air to be intact except for one wing. It had come to rest in a nose down position and one wing had been torn off on impact. There was no sign of activity around the crash site.

The rescue team was immediately dispatched and arrived at a lake near the crash site at about noon. The crash was located forty miles north of Goose Bay. The Norseman had crashed three miles from any lake large enough to accommodate the SA-16 Rescue Aircraft. The hike to the downed plane was through a muskeg and across two small ridges.

Three small lakes had to be skirted to reach the crash.

Both men in the plane were dead, apparently killed on impact. A closer inspection revealed severe damage to the plane – much more than had appeared from the air. The co-pilot's body could be removed from the plane but metal had collapsed and trapped the pilot by his feet.

This developed into a perplexing problem because the Rescue Team had no equipment to force the metal from around the pilot's feet. One member of the team was a close friend of the pilot and finding his long time friend dead and so trapped became an exceedingly emotional thing.

The team decided that in order to remove the deceased, his feet would have to be removed at the ankles. The only tools available were a small saw, a hunting knife and a small hatchet. To accomplish this morbid task would require someone to crawl into the crushed cockpit while others would hold onto that person's ankles. To complicate matters further, the body was covered with flies, swollen and stinking.

No one really wanted to be the person crawling into that cockpit. Matters were decided when the friend of the deceased insisted that he should be the one to remove his friend from the plane. No one argued the point and there were sighs of relief when he volunteered.

The smell was so bad that handkerchiefs were

wrapped around the face of the man who had to climb, head first, into the cockpit and those holding him had to do the same. Milton was sure that he couldn't have done what his friend was doing. Extracting the body from the plane took over an hour. An exhausted man, both mentally and physically, finally crawled from the wreckage and the dead pilot was removed and placed in a rubber pouch.

It was late in the afternoon before the team members reached the lake and the waiting SA-16 rescue plane. Everyone was exhausted from carrying the two bodies from the wreckage to the plane. The take-off was bad and for a moment it appeared the plane was destined to remain on the lake. The wind had dropped and the lake wasn't that long.

Everyone – including the pilot – held their breaths as the rocket assisted plane roared toward the end of the lake and then barely cleared the Spruce trees at the end of the lake. On landing at Goose Bay, Spruce needles were found wedged into the right out-rigger. It had been close. Only a highly skilled pilot could have safely flown the plane from that lake.

The Sergeant, who had cut his buddy from the wreckage, was quiet for the entire flight back to Goose Bay and hardly said a word to anyone and that night, he drank himself into a stupor. He very seldom drank and his fellow team members understood how he must have felt. It had taken more nerve than many of the team possessed to do what he did.

When working so close to death, one would start to realize the frailty of life, especially for those having to fly in the North Country where harsh conditions are unforgiving to the pilot who makes a mistake or is unfortunate enough to experience a mechanical failure on his aircraft.

Another plane crash that year was that of a C-82 Flying Boxcar. This plane flew from Presque Isle, Maine on the way to Greenland with a stop for refueling at Goose Bay. The weather was overcast with a light rain falling limiting visibility. The plane circled Goose Bay and as it turned to align with the runway, one engine started sputtering and lost power. The other engine started running rough (a pilot's worst nightmare). That particular plane could only lose altitude when flying on one engine with any cargo aboard. There was no way that the plane could circle and finishing lining up on the runway with the cargo load it was carrying

The pilot did his best to control the fast descending aircraft and as the plane dropped through the clouds, he noticed the Hamilton River under him and in the middle of the river was a long sandbar. The pilot turned and made a beautiful wheels-up landing and dug a long grove in the sandbar and finally came to a grinding halt amidst a shower of sand and water. The power switches were cut off and the ten men aboard made a hasty retreat from the downed aircraft.

The plane had crashed across from Milton's cabin. Within thirty minutes after Milton arrived at the crash, they heard the rescue boat motoring up the Hamilton River toward the crash site. Rescue had been alerted as soon as the plane had dropped off the radar screen.

The flight crew and passengers suffered nothing more than a bad scare and being shook-up from the rough landing. They were a happy and thankful crew after considering how the crash could have turned out. If the sandbar hadn't been there they would have landed in deep water. It would have been nice if all crashes had turned out like that crash.

The plane wreckage remained on the sandbar for several weeks until a landing craft from the Corps of Engineers arrived and disassembled the wreckage and hauled it away. Several natives visited the plane by canoe and boat. They were fascinated by the "Flying Box Car." And, of course, there was always tea and food at Milton's cabin across the river from the crash site.

Another crash with a happy ending was that of the Base's C-54 (DC 4) aircraft. This plane had been assigned to Goose Bay to haul needed supplies and other priority cargo from the States to Goose. One task assigned to that plane was a once per week flight to Halifax, Nova Scotia to haul eggs, bananas, and milk to the Base. The occasional fresh milk, bananas and eggs were a tremendous morale booster. Once or twice each week those foods were served in the Mess Hall.

One cold, snowy evening, shortly after dark, the plane vanished from radar over the frozen Goose Bay. It was returning from its weekly flight to Halifax. Immediately a search was started. The last fix on radar showed the plane to be about eight miles out.

Milton hooked up eleven dogs to his sled and started toward the bay and the crash site. The snow was deep, but with that many dogs he made good time and soon spotted a light out on the bay. The light was from a flare set off by a member of the C-54's crew.

At about the time Milton arrived to the crash site, the Base's new tracked vehicle also reached the site. The plane had experienced engine failure from contaminated fuel and icing. The pilot was in the landing approach pattern when the problems occurred and he couldn't keep the plane in the air. He landed on the four-five foot thick ice and skidded several hundred feet before coming to a stop. One wing was torn off and the plane suffered extensive fuselage damage.

After the plane came to a halt, the crew gathered survival gear and quickly evacuated the aircraft in case there was a fire. Fortunately, there was no danger of fire. Crash landing in deep snow usually quenches fire. However, the crew wasn't taking any chance of being caught in a fire or explosion.

This flight crew was lucky in suffering no injuries from the crash except for a few bruises. The main problem was that several men were covered with broken eggs, smashed bananas and free flowing milk. They did everything right in evacuating the plane and taking survival gear with them.

Once it was ascertained that no one was injured and everyone was out of the plane, and the fear of breaking through the ice into the cold water had not materialized, a shelter was erected a safe distance from the crashed plane. The crews fired an emergency flare every 10 minutes and were sighted by a Fighter Interceptor pilot flying over the area. The Interceptor pilot immediately notified the Base Control Tower and the search had begun.

The two flight crews aboard the C-54 had attended Milton's Survival School. They wrote a letter to the Base Commander expressing their appreciation for what Milton had taught them in the survival school. The letter stated that "they had done exactly what they had been taught, and because of the training received, they had confidence in their ability to survive." That crew had been very blessed in riding a plane down onto the ice and no one suffering an injury. Should the plane have crashed in the summer the outcome might have been very different.

Milton received a fast ride on his sled back to the Base. The leader followed the packed trail left by the tracked vehicle. The eleven dogs pulled the sled at a fast clip back to the dock area and then along the road to the cabin located a few miles on the other side of the Base. Never had his team performed so well. He was elated that no one was hurt in the crash of the C-54.

—14—

Bad Times at Goose and the Chaplain

The Air Force, after the start of the Korean War, increased the tour of duty from twelve months to eighteen months for Goose Bay. This extension lasted only for a short time before the Air Force reversed the original ruling and changed the tour length back to twelve months. While the extension was in affect, several tragic incidents occurred as a result of that ruling.

One week after the new ruling, an Air Force Sergeant committed suicide by diving under a log bridge that crossed a small stream near the Base. He left behind his clothing neatly folded on the bridge and a note expressing despair at the thought of spending an additional six months at Goose Bay.

Another man hung himself from a crane in one of the aircraft hangers. Again, his suicide note revealed despair attributed to the longer tour of duty. Unfortunately, many of the personnel assigned to Goose Bay spent too much time despairing and complaining about being assigned to an isolated Base without access to a town or city.

Most personnel, however, adapted to the situation and made the most of the tour. The Base offered various forms of recreation and educational services and opportunities. The Base area became a universe for most men assigned there and they made the best of an unpleasant assignment. Those who enjoyed the outdoors accepted the extension without compliant.

Two Air Policemen received a court martial for conspiring to inflict personal injury on each other so they would be sent back to a hospital in the States. When the length of the tour was extended, they decided to shoot each other in the foot so they would be returned to the States for treatment. Any personnel experiencing serious medical conditions such as a gunshot wound would be flown back to the States to a military hospital. The dispensary at Goose wasn't equipped to handle serious cases, except for emergencies.

It is difficult to believe persons would think of hurting themselves to evade unpleasant duties. The two men had walked into the woods near the road. One had a .22 caliber rifle and shot the other in the foot. The pain was more than the man had participated and he started yelling and sobbing. Finally, after he had calmed down he asked for the rifle to shoot his partner in the foot as previously planned.

The man who had shot him refused because it seemed that the action caused too much pain on his partner and he didn't care to experience the same. When the one man limped to the Infirmary and was questioned about the circumstances leading to the foot injury, he confessed all.

Both men received a court martial and returned to the States to spend time in the Fort Leavenworth, Kansas Federal Prison. Their wish to return to the States was granted, but not like they had planned.

Another man talked three other men into stealing a boat with him with the intention of motoring out of Goose Bay into Lake Melville and down the coast of Labrador past Newfoundland to the States. (It was 700 air miles to Boston) They stole a 25-foot boat in Happy Valley owned by a man named Sullivan and motored down the Hamilton River to Goose Bay. When daylight failed they anchored the boat near shore. The next morning they awoke to a broad expansion of mud. The tide had gone out and left the boat high and dry in the mud flats.

The men had failed to report for work and an inquiry was made to determine their whereabouts. Someone reported to Milton that the men had been seen in Happy Valley and a boat belonging to a man names Sullivan was missing. Acting on a hunch, the Base's C-47 was dispatched to fly down the Hamilton River to Goose Bay in an effort to find the missing men.

The plane soon located them in the mud flats. They were waving shirts to attract the attention of the plane. Not only were they stranded until the tide came in, but had been bitten all night by mosquitoes. The mosquitoes and gnats had made life miserable and they were more than happy to return to the comfort of the Base and whatever punishment awaited them.

The Base rescue boat was dispatched and with high tide, towed the boat back to its owner in Happy Valley. The men were court martialed and fined for their action. They had to pull Kitchen Police work – peeling potatoes, washing pots and pans and cleaning floors – for thirty days as punishment for their actions. Because of the problems the extension had caused, the tour was once more reduced to twelve months.

Several men turned to drinking heavily to pass the time at Goose Bay. The Base Clubs did a flourishing business from a group who persisted in becoming intoxicated whenever the money and opportunity would present itself. Many of these people were veterans of World War II who had remained in the Air Force after the war ended.

One night, the Air Police were dispatched to the NCO club involving a compliant about an old sergeant being drunk and eating beer glasses. That's right, eating beer glasses. When two policemen attempted to arrest the man, they were propelled out the door. They called for help and two other policemen arrived and still they were unable to subdue the passive intoxicated man. He just didn't want to be bothered and wanted to enjoy his beer.

Milton was on patrol and overheard the call for help over the radio. He responded and walked in the door as the man, backed in a corner, holding a cue stick in his hands threatened the four policemen. They couldn't get close enough to use their short clubs because of him yielding the cue stick. The incident was almost humorous.

Deadly force couldn't be used in such an incident. The man was bothering no one when the police had attempted arresting him. His only crime was eating a beer glass. Perhaps he could be considered attempting to destroy government property, namely, himself. The police didn't know how to handle the situation.

Milton recognized the Sergeant as a person who had fished with him on several occasions. He asked the Sergeant in charge of the police shift if he could try talking to the man because he knew him. Permission was granted and the police left the Non-Commissioned Officers Club and waited outside.

"Can I talk to you?" Milton asked the Sergeant who was holding the cue stick. The man squinted through red rimmed eyes and recognized Milton. In a slurry voice the man asked, "Is that you, Kid?"

"Put the stick down and let us sit at the table and talk." Milton told him.

"Sure enough," he replied.

The man told Milton that he had grown up in Germany and from an early age, with his parents, had worked for a circus. His act was to eat glass. To emphasize his point, the man reached over and took a bite out of a beer glass. He explained that he and his family were blessed with powerful jaws and teeth.

In a drunken voice he explained to Milton that the secret was to grind the glass between his teeth until nothing but powder remained and then swallow the powder. He did that trick often and had never suffered any repercussion ... not even a stomachache. Perhaps all the beer he drank with the glass helped him. He told Milton that he needed a ride to his barracks because he was too drunk to walk that far.

"I refuse to go with those other policemen, but you're my fishing buddy and I will go with you," the Sergeant told Milton.

Milton led the huge sergeant (He was six foot five and weighed almost three hundred pounds and most of the weight bone and muscle. He was the strongest man that Milton had ever met) by the arm out of the NCO Club and to his jeep. He informed the Sergeant in charge what the situation was and was given permission to drive the man to his barracks. Milton was told to stop by the Infirmary and have the man checked by a doctor.

The Sergeant was examined by a base doctor and found to have suffered no ill effects from eating glass. Milton and the other men were fortunate that the old Sergeant knew Milton from fishing trips. He would have been difficult to subdue without someone being injured. Milton was barely eighteen at that time. The man always called him "the Kid."

Another incident involving a drunken man was on a boat trip to the Traverspine River across the river from Happy Valley. Two boat- loads of Air Force men were invited to Bob Michlian's home on a Saturday morning. The boat ahead of the boat Milton was riding in suddenly swerved and a man fell out of the boat into the icy water of the Hamilton River. It was late May and the ice had just recently started to melt and moved out of the river and into the Bay.

When the boat Milton was on came to the spot where the man had fallen into the river, Milton dived overboard in a rescue attempt. All he could see in the clear water was the top of the man's bald-head. He dived down, grabbed him by the collar and surfaced.

The man started struggling and Milton was experiencing a dangerous situation. He had dove into the water wearing boots and heavy clothing. He found it difficult to keep afloat himself, much less, keeping the struggling man from drowning. Both Milton and the drunk Sergeant were saved when another man dove into the water and assisted him with the struggling man. One of the boats came near and they were helped aboard. All three men were shivering from exposure to the cold water.

Milton was disgusted to find that the man who had fallen overboard was so drunk he could hardly walk. Once the boats arrived to the dock, the man staggered from the boat and again fell into the water. This time a boat hook was used to drag the man to shore. He was dragged into Bob Michlian's house where he was undressed and put to bed to sleep off his drunk.

Milton often guided people fishing and camping. He was asked to take the Base Chaplain and his friend on an overnight fishing trip to one of the lakes near the Base. He was more than happy to do that. They had planned an overnight trip to the Alexander Lake area northwest of the Base. He knew the location of a small cabin near one of the lakes that contained plenty of trout.

The Chaplain discovered at the last minute that his fellow officer was unable to make the trip, but he decided to go anyway. It made no difference either way with Milton. One man would be easier to guide than two stumbling over themselves.

Chaplain Johnson told Milton that he had never camped before and was looking forward to experiencing trout fishing and camping. He was eager to learn about the outdoors. Milton packed two summer weight sleeping bags and basic camping items such as tea, a skillet and pot for brewing tea. He decided not to take any food and would treat the Chaplain to what it was like to live, almost, off the land. He carried the filled pack so that the Chaplain wouldn't be burdened with a load and could enjoy the hike.

After the truck had dropped them off at the end of the road, Milton and the Chaplain started the trek into the back lake. There were several small lakes in this particular area and the best fishing was in the back lakes. It was a two mile hike to the lake where the cabin was located.

Two lakes had to be skirted and the inlet to another lake waded to reach the cabin. The Chaplain was game, even if he wasn't used to hiking through such rough terrain, he did well in keeping up with Milton. The man was huffing and puffing by the time the cabin came into view. It is difficult for a man to sit in an office everyday and then head out into the outdoors where energy has to be exerted. He probably used muscles that he didn't realize he possessed.

The log cabin was located on a rise above where one lake emptied into another lake. It was constructed from unpeeled Spruce logs. There was one door and one window. The cabin was furnished with a table and two benches, a small wood stove and two army cots with old, not too clean appearing mattresses. The floor was packed dirt. Milton thought it a nice cabin but not the Chaplain. He looked around with apprehension at the crude cabin. His look seemed to indicate that he didn't like the accommodations but would make the best of a bad situation.

Milton had spent many nights in that small cabin during the winter and had appreciated it being comfortable and functional. The window and doorway looked out over a very scenic lake and a thick Black Spruce forest on the far side. Mountains could be observed in the distance. It was one of those million dollar views. It was the kind of picture that was on scenic postcards.

The Chaplain started asking Milton questions when they first arrived at the cabin. The first question was, "Where is the well?"

Milton told him that the water supply was from the crystal clear lake.

"Are you sure the lake water isn't full of bugs and is drinkable?" he asked.

Milton assured him that many survival students had drunk the water before without ill effect.

The next question was, "Where is the toilet?"

Milton pointed to the deep forest behind the cabin and handed him a roll of "important paper." The Chaplain didn't seem too pleased with the facilities and shook his head in disbelief. Milton wondered if the man thought there would be a hotel at the lake with servants and modern facilities.

Milton cut a supply of wood for the stove and just before dark took the Chaplain trout fishing. That was an exciting event. The Chaplain hooked several trout and was thrilled with fishing. None of the trout were over ten inches, but the Chaplain treated them like monsters. He was really thrilled with catching the fish and his spirits and attitude improved.

By the time Milton was finished cleaning the fish, darkness was upon them. Milton lit four candles in the cabin and started a fire in the stove to cook the trout and ward off the chill of the evening. Suddenly a loon cried it's lonesome call out on the lake and the Chaplain jumped up and blurted out, "What's that noise? Was that a wolf howling?"

Milton explained to him that a loon was a bird and that was its night call. His explanation seemed to satisfy the Chaplain.

At various times throughout the trip, Milton heard the Chaplain state over and over that he wished his friend George had been able to come on the trip. He indicated that he would enjoy the trip more if only his friend had been able to come. Milton figured that he wasn't much company for the Chaplain. Maybe it was because he seldom spoke unless addressed.

The trout and hot tea were a very satisfying meal to the two hungry men. The Chaplain told Milton that he never had the opportunity to live an outdoor life because of being born and reared in Atlanta.

He was interested in the outdoors. He had thought that camping, fishing, and hiking would be fun, but he wasn't having as much fun and enjoyment because his friend George hadn't been able to come on the trip. Milton grew sick and tired of hearing about "George."

The Chaplain read a copy of *Reader's Digest*

that he had brought along by the flickering candle-light. Milton went to sleep immediately and some-time during the night he was awakened by a shout.

He was a very light sleeper, so he was instant-ly awake and jumped out of bed with his .45 caliber pistol in hand to find the Chaplain up and shining his flash light around the small cabin. Milton asked him what was the matter and he replied "See them on the table. They're covering the table."

In the flashlight beam several small woods mice could be seen searching the tabletop for scraps of food.

The Chaplain yelled that the cabin was full of vermin. Milton didn't know what "vermin" meant. Not wanting to appear ignorant, Milton told the Chaplain that he didn't see any vermin.

"Sergeant," he yelled, "See them on the table."

All that Milton could see were six cute little mice chasing each other across the tabletop.

He replied that all he could see were some mice on the table. He didn't know about any "vermin."

"Sergeant," the Chaplain retorted, "Mice are vermin."

"Oh," replied Milton. Milton tossed his boot at the table top, scaring the mice from the table and went back to sleep.

Later in the night Milton was again awakened by the Chaplain yelling. Attempting to maintain and keep his cool, Milton asked the Chaplain what was wrong this time. The man replied that something was running across his sleeping bag. Milton shined his light around the cabin and discovered a weasel on the floor at the foot of the man's bed eating a freshly killed mouse.

Apparently the chase had crossed the Chaplain's sleeping bag. The man was terrified, and Milton was angry at having been awakened two times during the night. All he wanted was a good night's sleep.

The Chaplain lit all of Milton's candles and refused to return to his cot. He sat on top of the table with a stick of firewood in one hand and his flashlight in the other hand. Milton urged the man to go back to his bed. He attempted to explain that the mice and the weasel were harmless to humans. His reasoning fell on deaf ears. In disgust Milton went back to sleep.

Milton awoke at first light and found the Chaplain draped over the table sound asleep. Milton started a fire in the stove and placed the tea water on to boil. The evening before he had set a snare for a rabbit and had been successful. He cleaned the rabbit at the lake's edge and had it frying for breakfast when he woke the Chaplain to eat.

The man looked exhausted and after washing himself at the lake came in and ate breakfast with Milton. He seemed somewhat ashamed of his antics of the previous night. Milton explained to him that there was no way to keep the "vermin" (he felt proud to use a new word) out of the cabin and they were harmless. The Chaplain only shook his head and told Milton that he was ready to start the long hike back to the Base. He never asked Milton to take him camping again. And Milton was glad.

—15—

The B-24 Crash Mission

In late August 1952, a special photography unit from a Naval Base in the States did an aerial survey of hundreds of square miles around Goose Bay. The photographs revealed many shiny spots in the surrounding area that most likely indicated sites of plane crashes. One especially large spot on the photograph was observed to be in the Mealy Mountains about fifty-five miles from the Base. The best guess was that the shiny areas were reflections from metal. This would indicate a downed aircraft.

There was no record of a plane crash in that particular area. Dozens of crashes had occurred in areas surrounding the Base. Most dating back to World War II when Goose was a major refueling base for planes flying the great circle route. (Presque Isle, Maine, to Gander, Newfoundland or Goose Bay, Labrador, Greenland, Iceland, and Scotland)

Because of the limited range of many planes back then, especially fighters, refueling Bases were needed in ferrying planes to England. When such a wreckage was located, the rescue personnel painted a large "X" with orange paint to identify old crashes so they wouldn't be mistaken for a new crash site. The crash site in the Mealy Mountains wasn't marked as a known crash site.

Many planes vanished in World War II and considerable effort had been made since then to locate downed planes and identify the remains of the military personnel. Based on Air Force policy at that time every effort would be made to investigate any evidence of old crash sites. It was a national policy to locate, recover and identify crash victims regardless of when the crash occurred.

Milton was asked to help guide a team of thirteen men to the suspected crash site and identify the type of plane and recover any remains found there. To reach this downed aircraft, the team would have to be transported by the Base's tugboat about fifty miles out beyond Goose Bay and into Lake Melville to a point of land below the Mealy Mountain near as possible to the crash site.

The plan called for debarking from the tugboat at a point of land named the "Hare's Ears". The "Hare's Ears" consisted of two huge giant stones resembling the ears of a rabbit protruding from the shoreline, – almost awe-inspiring. Once there and ashore the team would cross four miles of deep woods, fording at least two creeks and then climbing a two thousand feet mountain. The mountain was steep, but there were plenty of ledges and rifts in the stone wall with foliage growing from the cracks. It would be a hard climb, but with little danger, if care was exercised.

The team spent the time during the long tugboat ride to the "Hare's Ears" talking and drinking coffee. Milton, Gene Cooper (A highly qualified member of the Ground Rescue Squadron) and Capt. Self, the officer in charge, talked and planned the mission. Gene was to ferry the men ashore using a cargo canoe, powered by a ten HP Johnson motor, and towing a rubber life raft.

Milton was to go ashore with the first load and using his compass, blaze a trail for the others to follow as soon as they were all ashore. Because of the roughness of the water, considerable time was required to ferry everyone ashore.

Once in the thick forest the mountain couldn't be seen until almost at its base. He had a twenty-five minute lead. The tug had stopped five hundred feet offshore because there was a danger of grounding on several large rocks located near the surface. If the tug would have run aground, the nearest help to re-float the tug would have to come from Newfoundland – several hundred miles away.

Because of the roughness of the water caused by a strong gusty wind, most of the men were wet by the time they landed. After the canoe and raft were safely stored on high land and securely tied to a tree, the team set out to follow the trail marked by Milton.

The first stream to cross was shallow and filled

with rapids, but Milton was able to place several large flat rocks in strategic points and everyone was able to cross without getting wetter than they already were.

When the team reached where Milton waited at the stream, he ventured ahead marking a trail while they rested. The next creek had a large Spruce tree blown down across its width and with care the team was able to ford the stream by walking on top of the slippery tree trunk. Some had narrow escapes when their feet slipped off the log. Some sat down and scooted across, ... perhaps feeling that caution was better than another wetting in the icy water.

The area was interesting because of the abundance of wild game that flushed ahead of them. There were fresh caribou and black bear tracks, and on numerous occasions grouse flew up before Milton. They were so tame that he could have easily killed some with his hatchet. Milton wished that he had the time to hunt and camp in that area. There was an abundance of trout in the streams they had crossed. But, there was no time for fishing or hunting.

The forest was so thick that the mountain couldn't be seen even though they were almost at its base, and then, suddenly the gray granite wall of the mountain appeared in front of them. The mountain loomed straight over them and Milton started seeking the best area to scale the steep edge of the mountain.

After a short walk he discovered a crack that ran at a slant up the face of the mountain. He started up the mountain and was joined by Gene Cooper. They stayed ahead of the rest of the team so they could pick the best possible path with the least danger. No ropes were used and if a person fell, in most places a ledge would have eventually stopped them. There were many small bushes growing from cracks in the rocks.

Milton was leading at about the five hundred - foot level when a tire-size boulder broke loose and fell. As the rock brushed past, Milton attempted to push the heavy stone with his left arm to hopefully divert it away from anyone directly under him.

The stone missed everyone, but the attempt at diverting the stone dislocated Milton's shoulder. The injury was painful, but Gene yanked Milton's arm and the shoulder popped back in place. Milton became nauseated in the pit of his stomach, but soon recovered and continued leading the rest of the way up the mountain. He was more cautious and examined each stone that even seemed like it could break loose. It was better to use caution than being careless and someone getting hurt.

The trip through the woodlands had been trying to the men because of the slippery moss covered forest floor. Also, gnats were out in clouds surrounding the men. But once they were near the top of the mountain a light rain started falling and cooled the perspiring men and dissipated the clouds of pesky gnats.

About one hundred feet from the summit, a small somewhat slanted flat area was located. It wasn't exactly flat, but flat in contrast with the rest of the steep mountainside. Since daylight was about gone, the decision was made to spend the night at that spot.

Each man carried personal items and a few packages of in-flight rations in their packs. One man had been assigned the task of carrying a very heavy radio for contact with a C-47 that was scheduled to drop sleeping bags, and later rubber body bags in the event any remains of the crew could be found. The radio was a World War II vintage set designed to be carried in a back-pack. It was very heavy because of the battery that powered it. The man packing that radio up the mountain had a very difficult time and needed help at times.

The problem facing the supply plane was heavy dark clouds causing bad visibility. The plane was contacted and the team could hear the sound of the motors as the plane circled in the general area. Darkness had almost set in before the plane could find a break in the clouds and make one low pass and drop the sleeping bags free fall.

Immediately after the bags were dropped, the weather closed in and the rain commenced in earnest. Two sleeping bags broke loose and fell to a ledge fifty feet further down the cliff. Milton retrieved the bags and gave one to Gene Cooper and kept one for his own use. All of the team members were too exhausted to eat. Everyone climbed into their sleeping bags, wet clothing and all.

Perhaps the greatest disappointment was that many of the bags leaked. The water proofing had apparently been removed from being dry cleaned after each of several missions. Milton was unlucky enough to have received a real leaky one. He removed his pack and field jacket and placed them under his hips in an effort to keep dry. That was a wasted effort because water continued to saturate the sleeping bag, which was like a sponge, and his clothing.

Milton had brought the only weapon on the trip. This weapon was his old- faithful parachutist folding stock .30 caliber carbine that he had lugged all over Labrador. In desperation, he positioned the carbine under his hips. This effort did allow the water to flow through his bag and under him. Needless to say, no one did more than doze throughout the long chilly night.

One major problem with sleeping on the solid rock ledge was that during the last ice age all the rocks were worn smooth by glaciers and had left few protective ledges to use for shelter from the weather.

All night, and it was a long night, it rained, thundered and lightened. The woodland and lakes far below their ledge, between the mountain and

Lake Melville, were illuminated like day. Everyone huddled in their wet sleeping bags and, perhaps some were praying that the bolts of lightning didn't strike them or even near them. The temperature dropped to about 40 degrees. That was the most intense lightning storm Milton ever had the misfortune to experience. That display of the forces of nature in action was awesome.

After the longest night Milton could remember, dawn ultimately arrived with an overcast sky and a chilled rescue team climbed out of their wet sleeping bags. The bags were so heavy from absorbing water that each had to be squeezed by two men before they could be rolled up and attached to their packs. The bags were still very heavy. As soon as camp could be made and fires lit, the bags could be dried before nightfall. Thankfully, the rain had stopped and the temperature had risen into the forties.

After a consultation between Milton, Gene Cooper and Captain Self, they agreed that Captain Self would, once they reached the summit, travel about one mile west and locate a small lake or stream with trees growing nearby to be used for firewood. There he would make camp and wait for Milton and Cooper to find the camp at the end of the day. They would be able to locate the camp by smoke rising from the campfires.

The top of the mountain was like a large Maple leaf. It was composed of ridges and valleys that resembled the veins of a leaf, and was mostly barren, with Caribou moss growing on many of the rocks, and there were rocks everywhere. Wild oats and other grasses grew around the many small ponds. Few trees could be seen except in low areas. Low waist high willows grew in the small valleys.

Milton and Cooper agreed to separate and search the area for several hours and then, before dark, walk north in hope of stumbling on Capt. Self's camp. After about an hour searching, Milton began finding small pieces of aluminum, and the further he walked, the more frequent metal was found.

Soon the trail of metal led down a rise to a small pond. There he found the forward portion of a B-24 Bomber's fuselage – from the wings forward– partially positioned in a small shallow pond. The pond was frozen ten months of the year and had been frozen when the plane crashed. The ice melted each summer. It was August and the ice had melted and the water was still ice cold.

Milton entered a broken section of the badly smashed fuselage and discovered three remains. The pilot and copilot were in their rightful positions. The fuselage was tilted to the left side. The three remains were dressed in heavy sheepskin flight suits and boots. The clothing had absorbed water and was very heavy.

The pilot was bent forward and to the left face down. The body was mummified from slightly above the waist and up. The body was frozen most of the year. His hair was gray with a crew cut. He was still a fine looking person. From his wallet, Milton identified his name to be Sam _____ and he possessed the total sum of one dollar in his wallet along with his identification card. The bodies didn't seem damaged in the least. No doubt they had been killed immediately on impact and thanks to the snow and ice animals hadn't bothered their remains.

The rest of Sam's body was a skeleton as well as that of the copilot and other crewmembers. The feet that had been protected in the sheepskin lined boots had been preserved and the flesh had turned green.

Outside the crumpled fuselage, Milton discovered the remains of three additional bodies. All that remained of two of the men were their bones. There was nothing remaining of their sheep-skin flight suits, no doubt those items of clothing were eaten by mice or larger animals. The bones had been scattered by animals, probably foxes or wolves. Both skulls were located, but some of the larger bones were missing. (In plane crashes, the teeth are one of the few means of identifying the deceased. The teeth are compared to dental records on file.)

The third body outside the crashed B-24 Liberator was found about fifty feet from the plane under a small rock overhang (Milton wished he had found such an overhang during the rainy night.) Apparently, this crewmember somehow survived the crash and crawled under the rock overhang where he opened a ration can and utilized a small rubber life raft in a futile attempt to build a shelter. His bones were under that ledge.

Milton searched the area surrounding the crash and found the crew's personnel records bound together and only the outside cover was damaged from the weather. Each record looked freshly typed like they were printed yesterday instead of years before.

He found a newspaper from Topeka, Kansas in a brief case inside the cockpit. The paper was dated April 4, 1944. There were also silk stockings and handkerchiefs in the brief case. The accident must have occurred two days after that date.

Later the plane was identified as a known missing aircraft. There was a lot of confusion resulting from all the flying activity of World War II. The plane had been reported missing on a flight from Topeka, Kansas to Labrador, on the way to Europe by the Great Circle Route. The plane had vanished in flight and after a short search, written off as many other planes at that time had been.

Milton walked fifteen minutes north and located smoke from campfires. The camp was situated in a small valley alongside a small stream flowing into a pond. The camp was using water from that small brook, which Milton had followed from the crash site to the camp. The rescue team was drinking water flowing from the small pond with the mummified body. After Milton gave them news about the crash, and the stream, they sought a new source of drinking water.

Gene Cooper arrived at camp about the same time as Milton. He had found some bits of metal, but not the crash site.

To everyone's surprise, Sergeant Buck Jordan arrived at the camp with about forty pounds of caribou meat. He was newly assigned to Goose Bay and to the Rescue Squadron. He had requested to come on the rescue mission for the experience. Buck had considerable experience big game hunting while stationed in Alaska.

Buck field-tested rifles for the Savage Arms Company. Once atop the mountain range Milton had loaned him the .30 caliber carbine because of all of the caribou trails crisscrossing the mountains. Buck had found a convenient spot overlooking a trail and after waiting for about an hour, three caribou had marched through a gap between the rocks and Sgt. Jordan selected one of the smaller caribou and dropped it with one shot through the heart.

The delicious caribou meat wasn't the only surprise awaiting everyone. While it was still light, the C-47 "Gooney" Bird circled and dropped a cargo parachute. When the parachute opened, beer cans rained down upon the camp. Early in the day, once camp had been established, Captain Self had contacted the support plane and request that five cases of beer be dropped for the team. Somehow, the shock of the parachute opening burst the bottom of each case of beer. The cans rained down on the camp and exploded when they hit the rocks.

One man had been in his sleeping bag when the plane approached and he had just stood up when a beer can impacted his sleeping bag where his head had been just moments before. Perhaps five cans of beer survived the impact with the ground. You could identify those who "just had to have" their beer each day.

Some of the men were frantically trying to drain any remaining drops from the smashed cans. The incident was very humorous, but could have proven deadly should someone have been hit by a beer can. Anyone injured that far out in the wilderness would be at a tremendous disadvantage. Imagine the difficulty of having to carry someone down the face of the mountain and to the tugboat. It would have been a very difficult accomplishment.

The caribou steaks were cooked in skillets with about a quarter inch of water. The fourteen men ate most of the meat in one day. Everyone slept well that second night of the mission. Perhaps everyone was trying to make up for the lack of sleep the previous night. Many of the men had been completely exhausted by the climb up the mountain and the lack of sleep the night before. Most of the team was along for the experience and to carry any bodies found at the crash site down the mountain. Most weren't used to such exhausting work.

Daylight saw everyone up and packed. Milton led the team to the crash where pictures were taken, bones collected and placed in body bags. The water soaked flight clothing was cut from the skeletons because of the extra weight. The service records and personal effects, including money discovered with the remains was properly recorded and bagged. Two .45 caliber pistols were also found in the wreckage.

Later the sleeping bags were all tied together and placed in a pile, wrapped in ponchos and left at the camp area. Perhaps an Indian would find the bags while caribou hunting and feel rich from such a discovery. There was ample sign of Indians having camped at that small pond in the past. There were a few empty cans and ashes from previous campfires. The team consumed the last of the remaining caribou before leaving camp.

At the top of the mountain, Capt. Self attempted to contact the plane that could be seen circling between them and the lake. The radio had apparently died and wouldn't pick up the airplane or the tugboat (The tugboat could be seen several miles away heading for the pickup point.) The air was so clear that one could almost see forever.

Capt. Self became so disgusted with the radio that he tossed it off the face of the mountain. It could be heard bouncing from ledge to ledge. The man required to tote the radio on the mission was relieved. He had felt like tossing it away a dozen times, especially when climbing the mountain with that burden attached to his back. The darn thing was a Forestry Set and weighed about thirty pounds. That was a lot of weight to have carried up the mountain.

Milton sought an easier route down the mountain because of the body bags carried by the men. Only one was extra heavy, and that was the bag containing Sam _____, who was partially mummified. All the remains were treated with the deepest respect. Milton sought an easier trail down the mountain to guarantee a safer descend.

Milton noticed markings on a rock and discovered an Indian trail descending the face of the mountain. The local Indians hunted caribou in the mountains each year and had for generations. Captain Self challenged his selection of a new way to descend from the mountain.

He wanted to return the route they had previously climbed and demanded to know why Milton was descending another way, which appeared further. Milton explained that the trail he had selected appeared to be a much safer trail to use by the men carrying the remains. Standing where they were and looking down was almost scary. From the top, the mountain appeared to drop almost straight down. When climbing and facing the wall, the mountain didn't look quite as steep as it looked from the top.

Capt. Self disagreed. Milton asked if he was

ordered to return by the same route he had followed climbing the mountain. Capt. Self told him that it was a recommendation, not a direct order. Milton politely informed him that he was using the Indian trail because it appeared a safer route to descend. Indeed, it must be a good route or the Indians would have never used that trail time after time as indications of use showed.

All but three men followed Milton down the mountain on the Indian trail. Even on that trail one had to be very careful. They arrived at the base of the mountain about one half mile from where they had originally climbed. They could see Capt. Self and the three men who followed him still about a thousand feet up on the side of the mountain. Climbing down such a mountain is much slower and difficult than climbing up.

Several times Captain Self had followed rifts in the mountain-side that led to drop-offs. They would have to retrace their path and attempt to locate a easier and safer way down. Eventually, they arrived exhausted at the foot of the mountain where Milton and the rest of the team waited by a fire drinking tea.

The tugboat was waiting for the men by the time the last one reached the shore. Everyone was tired and Capt. Self looked downcast and finally called Milton aside and apologized. He said that he should have followed the Indian trail too. Milton assured the Captain that he had done well for his first rescue mission and that selecting the correct descent from a steep mountain like the Mealy Mountain could be very difficult. The Captain seemed in better spirits after Milton told him that. That officer was a really decent man, and he had made a mistake. Many people are too ashamed or filled with pride to apologize when they make a mistake. Not this Officer! Milton had great respect for the man because of him admitting that he had been wrong.

Once aboard the tugboat the team was served a delicious steak dinner finished with coffee and apple pie. (The caribou steaks had tasted better) After that meal almost everyone found a niche to sleep for the return trip across the lake to Goose Bay. The water was calm and the ride smooth.

Capt. Self told Milton that forty thousand dollars would be paid to the Air Force from a fund established to pay the expenses of recovering bodies from planes lost during World War II. That was considerable money in those days.

When the tugboat docked at Goose Bay, Milton was given a ride to the edge of the high lands overlooking the trail to his cabin. It was good to be home once more.

—16—

The 54th Rescue Squadron

Goose Bay's Air Sea Rescue Squadron was instrumental in saving many lives in the North Atlantic. Often lost and disabled planes were located and directed to a safe landing by the efforts of navigators aboard the rescue planes kept on alert for that purpose.

When Milton first arrived to Goose Bay, a B-17 Bomber converted to Air Sea Rescue use, flew regular patrols between Labrador and Greenland. The bomber was fitted with a specially made rescue boat in its bomb bay to be dropped to survivors of downed aircraft or foundering ships and boats.

Because of the dangers of flying single engine planes on the great circle route, the bomber was in the air whenever flights of fighters flew to Europe. The presence of the bomber with the survival boat under its belly, ready to be parachuted down to crewmen in distress, was a comforting sight.

Soon SA-16 flying boats were added world wide to Air Rescue Squadrons. The plane was slow flying but could remain in the air for considerable hours with external fuel tanks. This plane could remain in flight for as long as a flight crew could endure the fatigue. It wasn't the most comfortable plane to fly in for long hours.

The SA-16 and crew was maintained on alert twenty-four hours a day. It was ideal for landing on the numerous lakes in Labrador and was capable of landing on the ocean too. This concept proved more efficient than the B-17 bomber conversion and soon the B-17s were a thing of the past. It was sad to see this relic from WW II phased out of service. This plane had been the backbone of the Air Force's Bomber Command during and through the war.

The following is an example of a typical rescue mission flown by a SA-16 from Goose Bay.

Little did Captain Durwood Matthews realize when he was in Navigation School at Coral Gables, Florida in 1942 that someday the techniques he was learning would be put to use in the skies over Labrador and the North Atlantic.

Capt. "Red" Matthews was assigned to the 54th Air Rescue Squadron and with his crew was on alert the night of July 22nd 1953. There was a beautiful display of Northern Lights and the crew had already made one flight to check on a survival team training on a river near Carter Basin that had not reported in by radio.

The SA-16 had circled the survival camp and made radio contact and found everything was fine. Because of the Arctic Lights radio contact with the Base had been impossible for the team on the ground. After returning to Goose Bay and reporting the group was ok, they turned in for the night, but only had time for a short nap.

Shortly after midnight the klaxon sounded an alert and the crew scrambled for the SA-16 sitting on the ramp.

Once airborne they received the details of the emergency. A Flying Tiger DC-4 en-route from Keflavik, Iceland to Gander, Newfoundland had lost one engine. The plane was carrying sixty-eight passengers (a small load by today's standards) and had already passed the point of no return. The plane was lost and another engine was running rough. The situation was becoming quite hazardous.

The SA-16 was to make contact with the DC-4 and escort it to a safe landing in Newfoundland. The problem would be to locate the plane by flying to a point where the plane should reach at a certain time based on its speed. The pilot, Capt. Roy, was a seasoned rescue pilot who had flown numerous missions using many different types of aircraft.

The problem of locating the plane would have to be solved by a difficult technique known as an off-set intercept and not on a collision course. This is a situation where one aircraft is flying between two points and the second aircraft has to depart from a third point and locate the first plane.

Accomplishing this task is difficult enough under ideal conditions, but weather conditions this night were far from ideal with the Northern Lights interfering with radio transmission. Only an expert navigator could plot and maintain a correct course for an intercept.

As the SA-16 gained altitude, calculations were made for an approximate position of intercept, bearing in mind that both planes were flying on different, but not opposite headings.

The SA 16 Rescue Plane had hardly gained cruising altitude while flying toward the coast when they encountered a thunderstorm that created an even more difficult situation. They attempted to fly around the thunderstorm and the plane became enveloped with "St. Elmo's Fire." At this point the radio operator became excited and wanted to bail out, even though at this time they were flying over the North Atlantic with water temperatures in the 30's that would mean almost certain death. He was afraid the "St.Elmo Fire" would cause the plane to explode. (This condition isn't completely understood and has caused many crewmen to panic when suddenly surrounded by fire.) They could see fire dancing off the wings.

After calming him down, Capt. Roy, the pilot picked up a signal from the plane in distress and wanted to alter course to intercept, but Capt. Matthews explained the situation and they resumed the proper course. If he had altered course the DC-4 would have been missed completely because of the speed it was flying.

Capt. Matthews gave the pilot the estimated

time of arrival for intercept and the SA-16 was closing in on the distressed plane but they were still in an area of scattered thunderstorms. Visibility was very poor.

At the exact intercept prediction, the co-pilot looked overhead and through some broken clouds saw the lights of the DC-4 and part of the problem was solved. It was only through the skills of an expert navigator and a dedicated crew that this intercept could have occurred.

At about the same time the Air Rescue SA-16 had left Goose Bay, the Navy had dispatched a P2V Neptune (Submarine hunter) aircraft from Argentia, Newfoundland on a collision course but it wasn't until after the 54th Air Rescue Squadron had made the intercept did they enter the picture. The rest of the mission was routine and a safe landing was made at Gander AFB, Newfoundland by the Flying Tiger DC-4 while the SA-16 returned to Goose Bay with a happy, but exhausted crew.

Capt. Matthews' superior navigation skills were credited with saving the lost and disabled DC-4. Many times during his one- year tour at Goose Bay, Labrador Captain Matthews was instrumental in locating lost aircraft by plotting a course that would take the SA-16 to the general area where help was needed.

Milton was really impressed with navigators like Capt. Matthews and Pilots like Capt. Roy, who were required to fly in weather that would normally ground most aircraft. Many lost pilots gained comfort and peace of mind when declaring an emergency and soon sighting the old SA-16 lumbering through the air and guiding them to a safe landing at Goose Bay.

Because of the SA-16s and their dedicated crews, many Pilots who had to bail out over the Arctic would have rescue on the way once they declared an emergency. Sometimes the SA-16s would land on small lakes and would barely have room to become airborne after initiating a pickup of downed flyers. One time, the SA-16 landed back at Goose Bay with tree leaves or Spruce needles lodged in their outriggers. Flying under such conditions required a pilot and crew with nerves of steel. One mistake would prove disastrous.

Sometimes the SA-16s would land in the ocean to pickup survivors from a boat sinking or a downed aircraft and because of the water being calm, or to the other extreme, the waves too high, would have a difficult time becoming airborne again. One such incident occurred northeast of Newfoundland during a storm when a Navy plane ditched.

Thanks to the skill of the navigator aboard the SA-16, the crash location was found and when the plane landed to pick up survivors, the water was so rough that the plane couldn't become airborne and had to declare an emergency. They had picked up ten survivors and because of the roughness of the water and the extra weight the plane couldn't gain sufficient speed to become airborne.

The plane taxied into the wind for over an hour until the storm subsided and the wave height dropped. Then it barely escaped the grasp of the ocean. Another rescue plane had arrived and circled overhead and if necessary, would have also landed. Fortunately, that wasn't necessary.

Many people owe their lives to the efforts of the Air Rescue units located worldwide. These crews took many risks in an effort to live up to their motto "That Others May Live." Such were the men of the 54th Air Rescue Squadron at Goose Bay, Labrador. They were the Air Forces' finest.

—17—

Marriage and No Extension

January 1953 came almost too fast. Milton was scheduled to return to the states in February after serving three years in Labrador. The tour of duty was one year and Milton had extended six months at a time until three years had passed. The years had passed too fast.

Northeast Air Command, with headquarters in Newfoundland had asked Milton if he would continue to extend indefinitely. At that time limits were imposed on the length of time a serviceman could stay in an overseas assignment. The ruling had been made to return service people from plush assignments in countries such as England, Japan and Germany back to the States. Some were remaining six or more years overseas. That rule was to be waivered in Milton's situation.

When Milton had married, he hadn't known about a regulation requiring servicemen in an overseas area to request written permission from their commander to be married. He had dated Frances MacKinney for a year before asking her to marry him, he had requested a ten-day leave and it had been approved.

To further complicate matters Milton knew of a commercial Canadian Airline that flew to New Brunswick and back twice a week. Normally, military personnel taking leave would fly to Westover, AFB, Massachusetts on a Military Air Transport plane. Milton and his intended purchased tickets and flew to Moncton, New Brunswick and then took a bus to Portland, Maine and there married. They wanted to be married in the U.S.

Milton and his bride enjoyed a short honeymoon in Maine and then when attempting to return to Goose Bay discovered that travel to that Base was restricted and special permission had to be obtained for them to return. Milton sent a wire to the Base Commander requesting permission to return to Goose Bay. Authorization was immediately given for them to return.

Once back at Goose Bay, Milton was told to report to the Provost Marshal. The chewing out that Milton received was something to endure. The Provost Marshal informed Milton of all the trouble he had caused by not requesting permission through channels to be married and then leaving the Base on a civilian plane.

For three days a search of the Base and Milton's cabin had been conducted in a effort to locate him. He couldn't be found on Base or off. Normally, a service member would have signed out for leave and then checked in at the Flight Terminal for a flight to the states.

Milton was often away from the Base for many days, but the problem was that he had signed out for leave, but never showed up at the terminal. That fact triggered a search for him. After he couldn't be located, someone happened to think of the civilian airline operating out of Goose Bay from the Canadian side of the Base. They checked the manifest and solved the mystery of Milton's disappearance.

"You have complicated things, your extension for over three years here is in question. It may be out of my hands," the officer informed Milton.

"We had planned on you extending indefinitely, six months at a time, and continue operating the Survival School and working as a Scout. I don't know what to do now. I will inform you when I find out what action is to be taken," he told Milton.

A worried Milton departed the Provost Marshal's Office. He wondered if he might be busted back to private from sergeant. Before he left the office, he was asked where he was to live with his new bride. Milton told him that the cabin would be their residence.

The responsibility of marriage soon became apparent to Milton when he had to cut and split enough wood to burn day and night. He now had more to think about than himself. But, It was worth it all. It was nice to return to the cabin and have his wife waiting him.

Everything came to a head one day in early October when Milton was returning to the cabin from gathering materials for Survival School mock-ups. He met three Colonels from the base on the trail. They were the Base Commander (Newly assigned), the Deputy Commander, and the Provost Marshal. They stopped and talked with Milton for a few minutes. They had been out to inspect his cabin to see how he and his new wife lived.

The trail had become too much for their jeep, so they had walked the last mile to the cabin. They liked the cabin. The bad aspect was that drinking water had to be obtained from the river flowing past the cabin and the toilet was an outhouse located one hundred feet in the rear of the cabin.

Milton met with the Provost Marshal the following day and received some bad news. He was informed that because of his rank of SSgt and the fact that he had less than four years in the service, he wasn't authorized for one of the few available quarters for married key personnel.

The officer told Milton that everyone wanted him to extend, but there was no way that the Air Force Regulations governing married members of the service could be satisfied under the present situation. However, if he sent his wife to the States he would be allowed to extend. There was no way that Milton would do that. The request, which had been approved by Headquarters Northeast Air Command, authorizing Milton to extend for an additional six months was torn up before his eyes.

The purpose of the visitation by the Base's ranking officers had been to see if the cabin could some how qualify as suitable off base quarters for married personnel. If so, there was a slim chance that Milton could have extended. There was no way that the cabin would suffice for legal quarters. The officers seemed genuinely interested in resolving the situation. Milton really appreciated their efforts.

"I'm sorry but you will have to return to the States in February," Milton was informed.

He accepted this statement without visual emotion. Inside, he knew he would miss the dog team, cabin and the opportunity for living at the edge of a large wilderness. He truly loved living in Labrador and the excitement and enjoyment of outdoor adventures and living.

"We appreciate the job you have done with the Scout assignment and with organizing the Survival School," the Colonel informed Milton. He also told Milton to make the best of the time remaining on his tour. Milton would be given fifteen days before he returned to the States to handle any unfinished business.

—18—

A Winter Trip to the
Mealy Mountains

Milton was scheduled to depart Goose Bay on February 1, 1953. He had dreamed of taking an extended dog sled trip across Goose Bay into Lake Melville and along the southern shore during the winter. Previously, his duties of Scout and Arctic Survival Instructor had kept him too busy for such a winter trip. However, he had traveled to Northwest River and to other areas around the Base on numerous occasions. But, somehow the mountains seemed to draw him like a magnet. He had been there in the summer to retrieve bodies from a downed aircraft and had always wondered what the mountains would be like in the winter.

Another obstacle reared its ugly head in the form of a Base regulation against service members taking trips such as Milton planned. Since Milton had been assigned to Goose Bay there had been four different Base Commanders and three different Provost Marshals. The new Base Commander and Provost Marshal had been briefed to some extent regarding Milton and his duties. But in their eyes

Milton was just another Airman and subject to the same base regulations as any other serviceman stationed at Goose Bay.

When he requested permission for such a trip, which would have to be approved by the Base Commander, the immediate answer was a big NO because it was too dangerous. Milton couldn't believe that he had been turned down. After all he had taught survival school for three years and had lived off base during much of that time.

Refusing to give in without a fight, Milton asked for an audience with the Base Commander and during his appeal to the Commander, brought up his background and told him that the previous Base Commanders would have surely approved such a trip.

Colonel Thomas mused over Milton's request and finally said to him "I'll approve your request, because, after all, you've been teaching survival and have received many favorable communications regarding your ability. There is no way I would allow anyone else from this base to take such a trip." Needless to say, Milton was elated that his request had been approved.

Milton's brother-in-law, Rev. Danny MacKinney was to accompany him on the trip. Danny had recently arrived at Goose Bay and really wanted to take a dog team trip. Perhaps the beautiful hazy blue tinted mountains attracted him too. The base motor pool personnel had already moved Milton's possessions from his cabin to Happy Valley. He and his wife would live with her family for three weeks before leaving for reassignment to Lackland AFB, Texas.

When men from the base motor pool had moved Milton and his wife's personal effects from the cabin to Happy Valley and to the base for shipping, they thought the move would be a simple operation. From the start nothing went right. The temperature was twenty below on the evening the motor pool had scheduled the move. Milton was working during the day in an effort to finish some duties that needed to be done before he left.

There was two feet of fresh snow on the ground and it had drifted to a depth of six feet in places. The two men who were to move Milton started from the motor pool with a large four-wheel drive truck. They turned off the main road to the trail leading to the cabin. They only drove about two hundred feet before the vehicle was hopelessly bogged down in the snow. The large tires and four wheel drive wasn't sufficient to overcome the deep snow. It had been a foolish effort to drive off the plowed main road and attempt driving through the deep snow. Besides the two feet of new snow there was all ready three foot of snow blanketing the ground.

The two men walked back to a guard post on the main road and called for a wrecker to free the truck. The huge wrecker managed to reach the stalled vehicle before it became hopelessly stuck.

Back to the guard post walked four men this time. They called the motor pool for assistance.

The motor pool dispatched one of the two tracked snowmobiles newly shipped to Goose Bay. Two men were in that vehicle. This team came to within a mile of the cabin before it threw a track. The men did nothing wrong up to that point. The cold and deep snow was too much for the tracked vehicle.

The Arctic Lights were flashing across the sky in a beautiful display that resulted in radio interference. They couldn't reach the base with their radio because of the Arctic Lights causing nothing but static on the radio.

The two men left the warm cabin of the snow mobile and walked the three miles back to the main road and the guard shack. Both men froze their ears badly and were later court martialed for not wearing proper clothing for protection from frostbite. The men were only wearing field jackets and regular fatigue caps without earflaps. That was perhaps the coldest they had ever been. Before this, when outdoors, they would always be in a warm vehicle. To many men stationed at Goose Bay, being away from the confines of the base in the winter was like being on another planet.

They had thought the warmth of the snow mobile cabin would be sufficient for that trip. They never thought the machine would break down and they would have to walk and be exposed to the sub zero weather. That was poor thinking on their behalf. The winter cold could be unforgiving to the unprepared.

"Prepare for the worst first" was a motto when considering survival in the cold. These men failed to use common sense when venturing out in the cold. They had never before left the confines of the base roads. The base's roads were always plowed during and after a snowfall.

The remaining snow mobile was immediately dispatched and failed to proceed as far as the first vehicle before the main spider gear snapped. The men in this vehicle were properly dressed and walked two miles to the main road without incident.

The Non-Commissioned Officer in charge of the motor pool personally took charge and soon arrived on the scene with a Weasel amphibious tracked vehicle and loaded all of Milton's personal property aboard, including his wife. The weasel easily drove down the riverbank onto the frozen river and started down river toward Happy Valley. Milton followed with his dog team, which he should have used from the start. At least dogs don't break down. The Weasel's engine started missing and stopped operating after traveling about a mile. Finally, after some anxious tinkering, the motor pool sergeant was able to restart that tracked vehicle.

They finally arrived at the main road by traveling down the frozen Hamilton River for about an hour. There, a truck was used to take Milton's personal property to the base for shipment to the States. He didn't own very much, but it had to be shipped or given away. He gave some of his things to a few of his native friends in Happy Valley.

Travel on ice by heavy tracked vehicles could be dangerous for those unaware and ignorant of ice conditions. Such an example occurred in March after Milton returned to the States. For training purposes, the newly repaired snowmobiles took a twenty-five mile trip to an area known as Carter Basin. This area is located at the base of the Mealy Mountains and across the lake from the Northwest River settlement.

They had the good sense of taking a native guide with them. When they turned from Lake Melville on to the ice leading into the Basin – several hundred feet – the native guide told the driver he was approaching bad ice. (Often an experienced person can detect bad or rotten ice by its coloration and knowing about the currents in an area)

The driver thought the ice looked good to him, so he continued toward the area the guide had warned as being bad ice. The guide jumped out of the snow mobile onto the ice and the snow mobile continued on some thirty feet until the ice gave way beneath the heavy machine. The four men in the snow mobile barely escaped through a roof escape hatch before the machine sank in thirty feet of cold dark water.

Fortuitous for that crew, the other machine

was following in their tracks some two miles behind. All they had to do was wait until it arrived. No one suffered injury or got wet from that incident. They were very lucky!

The following snow mobile picked up the survivors from the first vehicle and contacted the base and explained what had happen. They were instructed to continue on to Carter Basin where a survival camp had been established.

The native guide warned the driver to follow his instructions regarding which ice was safe. They safely circled around and drove past the area where the first vehicle had dropped through the ice. Again, the guide instructed the driver to take a wide berth around another area of questionable ice. The driver thought he knew more than the guide and drove into a section of bad ice. As dark water swirled around the snow mobile, the guide once more leaped through the escape hatch and onto safe ice.

The rest of the crew followed close behind him. The driver and the two men ahead of him exited the hatch and into the water and were quickly pulled out by the guide and other crewmembers. Water didn't completely soak them to the skin. Their heavy clothing prevented them becoming completely drenched for the short time they were in the water. It was a narrow escape from a sure death.

They were badly shaken from what had transpired. Both drivers were later punished for not following the guide's direction. He had been hired to prevent what had happened. It is difficult to believe that two snow- mobiles would break through the ice within two hundred feet of the other. However, even natives would sometimes misjudge the strength of the four to five foot thick ice. Sadly, Bob Michelin's son, Joe attempted to drive a dump truck from Happy Valley to Mud Lake on the ice. The truck broke through the ice, trapped the man in the cab and sank in deep water. He never had a chance to survive.

Milton returned from the base to Happy Valley in the early afternoon. He was elated that Colonel Thomas, the Base Commander, had finally granted permission for his trip to the Mealy Mountains. His wife and brother-in-law, Danny had packed everything and tied the bags and boxes to the sled in preparation for the trip. Seven dogs were hitched to the sled and they were eager to run. Immediately after a last minute check of the equipment that had been packed, they departed at a fast pace that soon slowed to a mile- eating trot. Milton would have preferred taking his time and thoroughly inspecting everything, but he and Dan were in a hurry to start. It was already late in the day.

The start of the trip went fine and late in the afternoon, just before dark, Milton stopped at a small trapper's cabin for the night. They were several miles from the mouth of the Hamilton River on the far shore of Goose Bay. The first task after stopping was to cut and split plenty of dry wood and then start cooking a mixture of corn meal and grease for the dog's food. Milton, as he did every night when on the trail, set out a few rabbit snares before retiring for the night. This effort resulted in two rabbits snared and waiting the next morning. The night was cold and clear. The temperature was a frosty 15 below zero. The small trapper's stove in the cabin kept them warm. The cabin or "Tilts" as the trappers refer to these small cabins positioned on their trap line a day's walk apart are very useful for travelers. Most are only about six by six-foot square. A bit crowded for two people, but better than sleeping outdoors.

They were up at first light. It was a beautiful morning with no wind and the sun cast long shadows from the trees out into the frozen bay. After a fast breakfast of biscuits, tea, and strawberry jam, the dogs were hitched to the sled and they were soon on their way along the shore of Goose Bay traveling toward Lake Melville and Carter Basin. During the night a large newly acquired dog had broken loose and wandered away. Two weeks later a trapper informed Milton that the dog had been caught in one of his traps about a mile from the cabin where they had spent the night.

Milton and Danny experienced some excitement when they crossed the mouth of a river that flowed into Goose Bay. The sled broke through the ice, but fortunately for them, the ice was "drum" ice. (This condition is caused when the bay and river have frozen and later water rises through cracks in the ice from the tide coming in and out. At high tide the water would once again freeze above the originally ice. This condition leaves a space between the firm and often very thick ice and the newly frozen surface ice.)

The sled crashed through the one-inch thick ice and dropped twelve inches to firm, thick ice. When this condition prevails, the situation isn't as dangerous as one might think. The initial crash through the thin upper section scares a person badly, and it is hard work reaching firm ice once again. After crashing and breaking through one hundred feet of drum ice, finally, firm ice was reached. An incident such as this is very scary. Crashing through the ice into the cold water is a very dangerous situation. The newly formed ice can be very sharp and easily cut the traveler's boots or mukluks. Milton had experienced that condition several times but never grew used to feeling and hearing the ice crashing under his feet.

The Carter Basin settlement (about six houses) is a village used only in the summer for a fishing camp. It is a strange feeling to be traveling through a wilderness area and suddenly come upon a village of two story white clapboard houses. Carter Basin is almost directly across Lake Melville from the Northwest River settlement. During the summer the natives would fish for Salmon and dry this delicious food for later use in the winter. Indians camp in that area during the summer and build canoes and dry the fish they have caught. The area is very scenic!

One of the houses was occupied, or at least one room was. A middle-aged lady was occupying the heated room. Milton stopped the dogs and he and Danny were invited in for tea. The warm room felt wonderful. The woman and her husband were living there for the winter. He was away checking his trap line. He was away fours days at a time.

The woman appeared lonesome to talk with someone. She informed Milton that a dog team from Happy Valley had passed there two hours previously, but hadn't stopped. (She wanted the latest news from Happy Valley.) The team ahead of their team was following an old Indian trail that ran from the far side of Carter Basin (about two miles) through six miles of forest to a stream leading inland to the Mealy Mountains.

Following this trail would save about ten miles of travel on rough ice hammocks exposed to strong winds. The Indian trail crossed a point of land that projected into Lake Melville. Traveling around that point of land on the ice was difficult and could be dangerous because of the ice ridges. The ice was piled up in huge piles of ice ten- foot high in places. Traveling with a dog team through such an area is slow, dangerous and very fatiguing.

After talking to the woman and drinking her tea, they returned to where the dog team was tied.

To their anguish the dogs had raided the food container and spilled the cornmeal and grease into the snow. The hungry creatures had consumed a large portion of the grease and trampled the corn meal into the loose snow. Milton was able to recover some of the corn meal mixed with snow. The loss of most of the dog food would become serious as the trip progressed.

Having another trail to follow made travel easy. Both were able to ride the sled. They were deep within the woods when darkness began to fall. Camp was made beside the trail under tall spruce trees. The thick forest broke the force of the wind.

They packed the snow where they intended to camp and covered the area with spruce boughs, and then a large sheet of parachute cloth was draped over a pole tied between trees. The small wood stove was quickly set up and a fire started. Soon snow was melting for tea water. Cups of hot tea quickly warmed a person on such cold days.

Another fire was started outside the tent to cook the dog's meal. This was a trying task because the cornmeal had to cook in boiling water for fifteen minutes, chopped up rabbits were added, and then the cooked cornmeal would have to cool sufficient for the dogs to wolf it down. Milton disliked having to cook the dog's food each day, but he realized it was necessary. He always carried a large pot on the sled for cooking the dog's food. It would have been nice to be able to purchase prepared dog food.

There was no such thing as commercial dog food available for the natives. Some natives would kill seals during the summer and preserve the meat in its own grease. Seal oil was the most stinking scent that Milton can remember from Labrador. Once the oil came in contact with clothing it remained and unless the temperature was extremely low the seal oil stunk to high heaven. Many people couldn't stomach the odor. Because of the odor, Milton never killed and preserved seals for dog food. Some of the natives who lived on the shore of Goose Bay or Lake Melville dried large quantities of fish to be used for dog food. The dogs would eat the fish, bones and all.

While the dog food was cooking several snares were set in hope of catching rabbits to supplement the dogs' food supply. It was only after the dog food was cooking and the shelter erected did Milton open the grub box tied to the sled to carefully inventory its contents. His wife had packed a beautiful food supply and unfortunately, only enough food for three days for two men.

There were three dozen uncooked biscuits between wax paper, two cans of peaches, cream of wheat, one can of condensed milk, one pound of bacon, and a quart jar of dehydrated potatoes. There was plenty of tea and sugar. Frances had baked Milton a large chocolate cake for a surprise. Opening the food box was indeed a surprise. They planned to be on the trail for eight days.

Milton felt like returning to Happy Valley then and there. It was his fault about the food and he didn't blame his wife. She was a new bride and thought she was packing plenty of food. Milton violated the survival motto of "Be prepared for the worst first." He knew better because he was a survival "expert."

For dinner they cooked three biscuits each on top of the stove and washed the biscuits down with cup after cup of sweetened hot tea. Before retiring to their sleeping bags, they each enjoyed a slice of delicious chocolate cake.

Sleep came late for Milton because he had to do some serious thinking. Common sense dictated that they turn back. If they were caught in a blizzard such as Labrador was famous for, the situation could become desperate. It wasn't unusual for one storm to drop two feet of snow. He was taking a chance continuing the trip without being properly provisioned. The temperature had climbed to about zero (very mild for Labrador that time of the year). Pride won and he decided to risk traveling without sufficient supplies. He should have stopped to realize that such an attitude had killed numerous people in Labrador over the years.

Daylight came with a beautiful sunrise and soon after a breakfast of tea and biscuits, everything was loaded on the sled.

The traveling was easy because of a hard crust on the snow and after a time they broke from the woods unto Lake Melville. Emerging from the deep woods on to a vast open expanse of ice was almost blinding. Soon their eyes adjusted to the brightness.

They met ten Indians pulling toboggans and sleds loaded with caribou meat. The Indians weren't too friendly, perhaps resenting others hunting and traveling in *Indian* hunting grounds. Generation after generation of Indians had established hunting and trapping grounds. They rightly resented encroachment by outsiders.

Milton stopped the dog team to allow the Indians to pass. His dogs didn't like Indians and he was afraid they might attack the men as they walked past. The dogs did attempted to leap toward the Indians, but Milton jumped on the backs of his leader and a front dog and held them. Danny secured the sled until the Indians passed with apprehensive glances toward the growling sled dogs. Milton never figured the reason why Indian dogs disliked white people and white people's dogs dislike the Indians. Milton thought that perhaps each race somehow smelled different.

The frozen stream they planned to travel on that would take them to the foot of the mountain was reached by early afternoon. Two natives were having tea over a fire build in an old Indian camping ground near where the trail again entered the woodland. Milton stopped the team and talked to the men and had tea with them. They were caribou hunting and planned to climb the mountain early the next morning. The men extended an invitation to hunt as a team with them. The veteran native hunters knew the trail that led to the top of the mountain where caribou lived during the winter months.

Because of the deep snow in the winter, caribou migrated to the summit of the Mealy Mountains where the snow was less deep because of the barren surface that allowed the prevailing wind to pack the snow. There was ample food for the caribou on the rocks atop the mountain.The caribou would paw the snow from the rocks and eat a special type of moss growing there, ... Appropriately named "Caribou Moss." That moss was edible for humans under survival conditions. It had little if any taste, but was supposed to contained vitamins that were good for a person attempting to survive.

The men told Milton to follow their trail up the frozen stream and across a large swamp and muskeg where the stream originated and make camp at the base of the mountain. The snow covered blue-tinted mountain could be seen looming above them in the distance. After the conversation the two men depart for the mountain where they would make camp.

The point of land where they stopped was an Indian camp grounds that was used mostly in the summer. There was an elevated cache with a few caribou parts, mostly bones, stored for future use. Milton allowed Danny and the dogs to rest for a time so the other team would have considerable lead to keep the dogs from catching up to that team and attempt a fight. Sometime it seemed that sled dogs lived for the opportunity to fight.

After traveling at a leisure pace, they soon arrived late in the afternoon at the base of the awesome, bluish tinted Mealy Mountain. Milton and Danny erected their camp about two hundred feet from the native's tent. Still, the dogs spent the night howling at each other and would have liked to break loose and start a real brawl.

Cooking the dog food took longer because dry firewood wasn't available in any quantity. The corn meal was getting dangerously low. They had caught three snowshoe rabbits in snares the night before. The rabbits were chopped in pieces and cooked with the corn meal, fur and all. The dogs could eat fish or rabbits, bones and all without ill effect. The shortage of dog food would eventually weaken them.

After the dogs were fed, Milton and Danny visited the natives and drank tea with them. The two men had a very warm tent. It was made from a special heavy canvas. On a scale of one to ten, Milton's tent would rate as a two compared to their tent's ten. Plans were discussed about the next morning's hunt and climbing the mountain by means of an Indian trail that led from ledge to ledge. The two men had hunted that area before and knew the trail up the mountain.

The climb was very dangerous. One slip on the

snow and icy face of the mountain could result in sliding from ledge to ledge all the way down the mountain. Milton slipped a few times, but caught bushes to halt his fall. His sealskin boots were very slippery on icy areas. Milton didn't attempt to lead the party up that trail. He depended completely on the two natives' knowledge.

The men had started climbing up the face of the mountain at first light. Snow shoes and rifles were strapped on backs to allow hands free to grasp bushes to assist in climbing about one thousand feet. The climb was accomplished in about two hours, thanks to a well- marked trail left by Indians who had hunted there since the last snow. Milton was beginning to think the area was becoming crowded. The climb was awesome and somewhat scary.

The natives intended to kill as many caribou as possible and then bring their dogs up the mountain to tow the slain caribou to the edge of the mountain. Then they would lower the deer from ledge to ledge until they reached the foot of the mountain. That was a very ambitious plan IF they could kill a few caribou.

Once on top of the mountain, Danny went with the older native to hunt and Milton went with the younger native to another area of the mountain. Walking was easy on the packed snow. Milton soon discovered that the native he was paired with wasn't a careful hunter. Apparently, he spent too much time around the base and had lost some of his hunting skills.

Milton spotted caribou tracks leading to a small canyon. Joe, the native he was with, wanted to rush down the trail following the tracks. Milton finally talked him into crawling to the edge of a small knoll so that they could carefully observe the depression that wasn't over one hundred yards wide with trails leading down into a further small valley between hills. There was no cover because the land was barren.

Milton crawled to the edge of the hill on the packed snow followed by Joe. He sighted several caribou under the hill and motioned for Joe to select one and he selected another. Milton expected Joe to continue lying in the snow beside him. Instead, Joe leaped to his feet, and fifty feet away, unseen behind several rocks, stood two caribou. If they had waited, the two animals would have walked in front of where they were reclined. Probably no further than thirty feet from them.

The two caribou snorted, scaring Joe badly, and alerted the rest of the caribou and they bounded over the hill. Milton shot at the retreating caribou and wounded one. It was a snap shot and he had no idea where the 30.30 bullet struck the moving creature.

Milton and Joe followed the blood trail of the caribou for several hours and came to the realization that the caribou could out walk them any day.

The wounded caribou kept up with the rest of the herd, so it hadn't suffered too badly from its wound. Besides, they were becoming tired. The sky was clear and a light wind was blowing. The temperature was about ten degrees. It was warming up and when that happened a snowstorm could develop. Perhaps the reader has been wondering how Milton knew the temperature. He carried a small thermometer when him when he traveled. Knowing the temperature is very important so that he wouldn't be surprised by low temperature and get frost bitten.

At the suggestion that they start back to the head of the trail leading down the mountain, Joe immediately took the lead. After a time Milton became suspicious of the direction they were traveling. What made him suspicious was the wind blown snowdrifts. The prevailing wind blew from the Northwest. The snowdrifts indicated they were traveling to the South. There was no human habitation within one hundred and fifty miles in the direction they were traveling. Continuing in the direction they were traveling would lead only to the Gulf of St. Lawrence.

He mentioned his suspicion to Joe, who immediately became angry and on the defensive and stated that he was a native and had lived in the area all of his life, and he knew that they were traveling North toward the trail head at the top of the mountain."

Milton pulled out his beat up old compass and discovered they were definitely traveling South instead of North. He told Joe that he was going to follow his compass heading. Joe attempted to argue, but Milton could be stubborn at times. He started walking toward the North and Joe finally turned and followed him. He pointed out to Joe that even the snow ridges created by a prevailing Northwest wind verified that he was correct in traveling the direction he was going. The native then conceded that he was wrong and was willing to follow Milton. Without the compass, the northwest prevailing wind verified that Milton was correct in traveling the direction he was going.

It was dark by the time they reached the trail that led from the mountain to their camp. Danny and the other man were waiting for them. Danny was in good physical condition, but he had reached his limit when he had followed the old native around for the entire day without food or hot drink. Walking on snowshoes, especially when not conditioned to such activity can be extremely tiring. Danny and his hunting partner hadn't sighted a single caribou. Apparently the Indians had hunted that area and scared the caribou.

Dan was sitting on his snowshoes not saying a word. He had done well on the trip, but he wasn't used to that kind of travel and living. He had finally played out. He was totally exhausted. It is difficult to think of Danny becoming tired like he was.

He was always so active.

While they were preparing to climb down the mountain, the sky cleared and a most beautiful display of Northern Lights swished across the sky. The moon was full and because of the snow, it was as bright as day. It was a scene of beauty unsurpassed anywhere.

A person could see the several miles down to Lake Melville like in daytime. Milton noticed a small black dot on the ice and the native identified it as a sled and dogs. He thought it strange for some one so far out in the wilderness traveling at night. Dog sled travelers would have stopped and made camp at the end of the day. A tent would have to be set up and the dogs fed.

The slide down the mountain, from ledge to ledge was quite an experience. It was an experience that Milton didn't care to repeat. The situation appeared unreal in the bright moonlight. Danny somehow made it down the mountain. Milton carried Danny's rifle and snowshoes as well as his own. When they arrived at the tent, Danny immediately crawled into his sleeping bag clothes and all. He was too tired to drink a cup of hot tea. No one had eaten since before daylight that day. In the Arctic food is very important. Think of your body as a furnace and like a furnace, when it has no more fuel it goes out. The cold saps a person's strength if there is no food to eat. Six thousand calories is considered the minimum intake when living outdoors in the

Arctic.

While Milton was cooking the last of the corn-meal for the dogs, he observed a circle around the beautiful full moon. A circle around the moon was a sure sign of bad weather to come. The bad weather could only be snow. (The closer the circle to the moon, the sooner the bad weather would arrive.) That sign always proved reliable in that part of the North. The temperature was still rising and was a warm 20 degrees. The circle around the moon and an increase in temperature was a sure sign of an impending snow-storm. Those conditions always proved reliable in predicting weather changes.

Morning arrived too soon. During the night the temperature had warmed up into the upper twenties. That was warm weather for January in Labrador. A few light snowflakes were falling. Milton and Danny broke camp and packed everything on the sled. Danny felt much better after resting all night and eating a big breakfast washed down by many cups of hot tea. Milton wanted to be out of the deep woods before the snow became heavier and made traveling difficult.

They visited the native's tent and drank several cups of tea with them. The men thought a big snow was coming. They were snug in their tent and besides, they wanted another day of hunting caribou. Also, they weren't feeling too good. (Two weeks after returning to Happy Valley, Milton discovered that the men had come down with the flu and stayed in their tent for an additional week until they felt like traveling back to Happy Valley.)

By the time Milton and Danny reached the shore of Lake Melville the snow was coming down in wind-driven sheets. Milton quickly made camp with the parachute material he used for a tent and lit the stove.

Fortunately for them, the Indians who had camped in that area at various times had several piles of dried wood on a rack to keep the wood above the snow. Danny cut and split a supply of that wood to a size to fit into their stove and stacked it inside and out of the tent. They wanted to be prepared in the event it snowed all night.

They were soon warm and lying in their sleeping bags on each side of the stove. The wind intensified and a wall of the tent flared out into the wind filling the tent with snow. Milton jumped outside and tied the bottom of the tent to two small logs and packed snow over the logs. Danny cleaned the snow from inside the tent and out of Milton's sleeping bag. The dogs were already buried under the fresh snow.

Only one other incident occurred during the night. It was almost humorous, but could have been serious. Milton was sleeping in his shirt and pants. The pants were made from canvas lined with a woolen army blanket. He filled the stove full of wood and went to sleep with his rear end out of the sleeping bag and near the stove.

He woke with a searing pain in his butt. He jumped outside the tent and sat in the already deepening snow. The rear of his trousers were charred. Another moment they would have flamed up and he would have been in trouble. He suffered no more harm than he would have from a bad sun - burn. That incident was almost humorous, except that it was very painful. Milton realized that under certain situations he could move fast. That was one such a situation.

The men awakened the next morning to deep snow and a roaring wind from the Northwest. A full size blizzard was raging. Milton's worst fears had become fact. There was nothing to do but stay inside until the blizzard blew itself out. Late in the afternoon the snowing stopped, but not the wind. Over thirty inches of snow had fallen and the temperature dropped to thirty-five below zero.

Late in the afternoon when the wind finally dropped and they ventured outside to a world of deep snow, Danny spotted a large Snow Owl sitting on a dead snag and shot it.

Food was dangerously low and they thought that owl would be better than nothing. Unfortunately, several dogs exploded from the snow when the rifle was fired. Two had gotten loose. One grabbed the owl and ripped it to shreds while another dog rushed into the tent and gulped down the one small piece of remaining bacon.

The other dogs had no food that night. There was no way to snare rabbits in the deep blowing snow. The men drank tea and ate the last four biscuits. A small jar of cream of wheat had been found in the grub box and that was saved for the next morning. They kept the fire going all the night and rested well.

Because of the shortage of food, Milton made the decision to cross a thirty- mile section of Lake Melville to the Northwest River settlement. Instead of following the shoreline and then traveling directly across the lake, he decided to travel at an angle directly toward the settlement.

At daylight, the reluctant dogs were harnessed to the sled and Milton started breaking trail toward the Northwest River Settlement. The snow was so deep that breaking a trail for the dogs and sled was very difficult making traveling slow and tiring. One dog hadn't survived the night! They walked until eleven o'clock that night without food or drink. Danny was excessively tired, and the dogs were about played out. Milton stopped and made camp on the ice. At noon Milton had attempted to start the small gas primer, one burner stove that he had brought along on the sled. He thought that a cup of steaming hot tea would be welcomed and give them strength. To his disgust and as hard as he tried, the stove wouldn't start burning.

The four snowshoes were stuck in the snow and covered with the parachute material and snow packed around the tent to keep the wind out. Milton's toes had started freezing through the skin boots he was wearing and his fingers to the first knuckle had frozen when he had tied the tent down the previous night.

For added warmth, they took boards from the sled for insulation from the snow and brought two dogs into the tent for extra warmth.

The tent was getting cozy for a time until the dogs started fighting outside and the two dogs inside the tent leaped into the melee, taking the tent with them. It was difficult getting up in the cold and rebuilding the tent. All during the night Milton had to massage his toes to keep them from freezing. Needless to say, that was a miserable night.

At dawn camp was broken and they started traveling toward an off shore island near the settlement. During the night the dogs had eaten Milton's camera and exposed its film and other film stored on the sled. There went the record of their great adventure in the Mealy Mountains.

The dogs were so weak from a lack of food that they could barely pull the sled. Milton and Danny had to hook themselves to the sled and help the dogs keep the sled moving. That was one incident when the dogs didn't try to fight each other. The noble beasts were completely exhausted and hungry.

Soon, only Milton and two dogs were doing any

pulling. Danny and the remaining dogs could barely place one foot or paw ahead of the other. At about two o'clock an island off the mainland on the far side of Lake Melville was reached. They could see houses in the distance at the Northwest River settlement. So near, yet so far!

Milton was so weak that he couldn't wield his hatchet and cut wood for a fire. He managed to push dead branches from the trees with his body. Lighting the fire was very difficult. He couldn't will his fingers to hold a match so it could be lit. Finally he stuck a match between his fingers and managed to light it and got the fire going. The ends of his fingers felt like pieces of wood.

The fire was a lifesaver. His fingers burned terribly when he warmed them before the fire. Danny was so tired that he could only sit on his snowshoes and lean against a tree. For someone not used to the harshness of extended dog sled travel, he had held up remarkably well. He was in good condition and neither smoked or drank. He was recently a college student and not used to the rigors of the North. Milton had been living out and traveling by dog sled for almost three years and was well conditioned for such hard travel and living.

Milton filled the pot with snow and melted it over the fire until it was warm and they drank that. The warm water helped them feel better immediately. Somehow, Danny and the dogs walked the final three miles to the mainland and to a native's home where Milton often stayed when he visited Northwest River. He normally paid the family $1.00 for each night he spent with them, That was the amount they wanted for the use of a bed. That seemed too low, but a dollar was a lot to people who had no money.

The wife of Milton's friend was cooking a caribou stew. She placed food before them until they were completely sated. Their meal consisted of a large cake, the pot of stew and eighteen cups of hot tea each. Dan went to bed and was immediately asleep and didn't awaken until late the next morning.

Milton was able to buy seal meat to feed his hungry dogs. He allowed them to eat all they wanted, feeling they deserved that and more. Milton went to bed at the end of the day and slept until the next day.

Danny woke with a severe stomach ache. He wasn't used to eating so much food at one sitting like Milton and the natives. Milton could go without food or survive on little food for two days. And then when food was available he could eat until he was stuffed and it didn't bother him.

The only notable effect of going without food was that weakness would slowly develop. The extreme cold would sap the strength from both men and dogs. He and Danny had been so hungry that they could have eaten about anything. If they had sufficient food for themselves and the dogs, Milton would have never suggested the long trek to Northwest River. They would have stayed in the tent until conditions were better for travel. Then they would have retraced their trail back to Happy Valley.

Because of the severe blizzard there were concerns regarding Milton and Danny surviving. Authorities from the base had radioed the Hudson's Bay store in Northwest River settlement requesting information from anyone sighting Milton and his team. The radio operator was able to contact the base with the news that the travelers had indeed survived.

Because of the blowing snow a search by aircraft would have been useless. The ground was obscure from the air all day. The blowing snow cut ground visibility when looking from the air to about twenty feet above the surface.

The temperature had dropped to thirty-five below and the thirty inches of fresh snow was blowing into drifts from the thirty to forty MPH wind. A combination of low temperature and a strong, gusty wind made the temperature more like sixty degrees below zero. Milton received his first frost bite after living at Goose for three years. Three spots on his face were frozen because of walking into the wind with no way to entirely protect his face. And of course, his fingers suffered frostbite.

Milton and Danny were the first who had spent the night in the middle of Lake Melville under such conditions and survived. Milton was thankful that they were able to endure those harsh conditions and still be able to walk. His survival training and good physical condition had been the key to survival.

He admitted that many things were done incorrectly. The shortage of both human and dog food was the main shortcoming of the trip. Had they had sufficient food for the dogs and themselves, they could have stayed in camp until conditions became better for travel.

Two nights were spent at Northwest River recuperating and on the morning of the third day they loaded the sled for the trip back to Goose Bay. Northwest River is located on a point where Grand Lake empties into Lake Melville. The river was 500 feet wide. At certain points the river was never safe for crossing because of rapids and a swift current. It was always better to circle out into the bay before crossing. Because of the swift flow of the water freezing came late and often the ice was eroded from underneath.

Milton's dog team was fresh and well fed because of two nights of rest. They were eager to travel. Danny was still feeling rather badly, but he wanted to travel the remaining twenty miles to his home.

The men and dogs departed the native's home where they had stayed and the team immediately turned and started across the Northwest River. Both men were riding the sled. Dan was in the sled and Milton was riding the runners. Apparently, they had started to cross the river at the wrong place because the ice started breaking behind the sled and steaming dark water boiling up behind the sled runners.

The Indians camped on the far shore came out of their tents and raced to the shore to watch the crazy American break through the ice. They started cheering and beckoning Milton to move faster, and he in turn, urged the dogs to travel faster. Somehow they made the other shore without the sled breaking through. One of Milton's feet had gone into the water up to his knee, but the fast pace of the team had jerked him from the water. The temperature was about zero that day. That was a warm day compared to the previous several days.

Looking back once they were on the shore, Milton could see the trail the sled had made crossing the river. Water was still boiling up and spreading in the snow and ice, and freezing immediately when exposed to the cold. Apparently they had crossed over rapids that constantly undermined the ice. He was very thankful for not breaking completely through the ice.

After that narrow escape the rest of the trip was uneventful. Danny rode the sled and Milton ran behind and occasional rode when the trail was good. They arrived at Goose Bay after about three hours of travel. The rest of the journey to Happy Valley was easy sledding. The roads were packed with snow and the dogs were at their best all the way to the Valley. It was remarkable how fast the dogs could recover from the ordeal they had experienced.

Returning to a warm house, no matter how humble, and to tasty food was welcomed. Both Danny and Milton were happy to have finally returned from their trek. Milton enjoyed teasing his wife about the food she had packed for them. It had been sufficient for two men about three days. They had been away for eight days and nights. All's well that ends well!

****

Two days after returning to Happy Valley, the mystery of the sled they had sighted the night before the snowstorm from atop the Mealy Mountains was solved. That slowly traveling sled on the shore of Lake Melville was that of an Eskimo who was experiencing a very difficult time. He and his family lived in a small shack on the outskirts of Happy Valley.

The man and his twenty-three-year-old son had departed Happy Valley four days before Milton and Danny had left. They were to hunt caribou in another area of the Mealy Mountains about one day's travel beyond where Milton had hunted. Their hunt had been successful. They had killed four caribou and butchered and wrapped the meat in canvas and caribou skins, it was packed and tied on the sled.

The father and son stuffed themselves on caribou meat before retiring for the night. They were elated at the ease of locating and killing the caribou. The next morning when Dan Knun woke, he was surprised that his son hadn't stirred from his sleeping bag. He good-naturally shook and attempted to awaken him. To his horror, he discovered that his son was dead. They were about forty miles from home. The man was overcome with grief. At first he sat staring into space, not knowing what to do. Perhaps he was thinking that soon he would awaken and it would all have been a nightmare.

Finally, he realized that he had to take his son's body back to Happy Valley. He tied the sleeping bag closed around his son and placed and tied him on the sled atop the caribou.

At first everything went well and he made good time. The snow was packed and crusted from the wind that had been blowing from across the lake. Overcome with grief, he didn't consider stopping and making camp for the night. All he wanted to do was haul his son's body home. The thought of making camp with his son dead and tied to the sled was too much.

He noticed the ring around the moon on that bright moon lit night and realized that a storm was approaching. He traveled into the night until the dogs became too tired and he had to stop and allow them to rest. He was hauling a very heavy load on the sled, including the body of his son. He finally stopped and erected his tent in the shelter of tall spruce and fir on the shore of Lake Melville. Snow had started falling by the time he made camp.

The man finally drifted into a troubled sleep and was awakened by his dogs howling. One of the dogs had gotten loose and was tearing at the sleeping bag encased body of his son. He almost beat the dog to death and retied it to a tree. The dog had managed to rip the cheek of his son's frozen head. He recovered his son's exposed head and suffered through the terrible storm until it finally stopped.

The man was forced to break trail ahead of the dogs and sled because of the deep snow. The dogs would often leap back at the sled and tear at his son's body. He used his ax to beat the dogs from his son's body. The dogs seemed frantic to attack and tear at the sleeping bag containing his dead son. The bag was soon in shreds from the dog's lashing fangs.

Once he had fought off the dogs, he chopped one of the caribou into smaller pieces and fed the dogs all they would eat, hoping the dogs would be too filled to bother his son's body. Feeding them the meat seemed to appease the dogs and they continued to follow the trail he was making for them to follow with the overloaded sled. Eating such a large quantity of caribou flesh made the dogs sluggish and made pulling the sled more difficult and very slow.

The poor man was afraid to stop and make camp. When night came, he was too tired to walk another step. His anguish-filled mind knew that he needed to rest. He stopped and fed the dogs more caribou and packed the snow next to the sled and placed his sleeping bag there so that he could sleep next to the sled and protect his son's body should the dogs once again attack.

He securely tied each dog to a tree to prevent them from attempting to attack his son's body while he attempted to get some rest. Breaking trail in deep snow all day was a very fatiguing task. It was a task that most men could endure under such conditions for only about two to three hours, and he had been breaking trail in the deep snow for eight hours. He had eaten nothing all day.

Later in the night he was awakened by a noise and found one of his dogs chewing on his son's body. He shot that dog without hesitation. The dog had chewed through the sealskin braided rope and gotten loose. The next two days were terrible for the emotionally-drained grieving father. The dogs became increasingly more aggressive and would boldly, as a team, rip at the body. Beating them with his sealskin whip was effective at first until it broke into several pieces. His arms became badly slashed from grabbing the dogs by the neck and tossing them away from the sled. Again and again, he was able to fight the dogs away from the sled and gain a few more miles on the trail toward Happy Valley.

The struggle lasted for two more days and nights until he was completely exhausted. Finally, he reached the mouth of Hamilton River where he was discovered by another native traveling by dog team through that area.

He was found positioned across his son's body with a 30-30 rifle in his hands and three dead dogs in front of him. He was sobbing uncontrollably and it was with difficulty that the other native was able to take the man's rifle and calm him.

The man's son had been badly mutilated around his face and head. A closed coffin funeral was held in the small church in Happy Valley. The father's hair had turned white almost overnight. Indeed, he had experienced something most difficult to cope with. The man slowly recovered from his ordeal, but he was never the same after that incident. Before the trip and the tragedy, he was always smiling and telling jokes. The trip changed his personality completely. He seldom smiled, never joked, would look toward the Mealy Mountains and get a dreamy sad look on his face. Perhaps he was reliving the time when he had lost his son and the ensuing events. To the best of Milton's knowledge, the man never undertook a hunting trip to the Mealy Mountains again.

Danny MacKinney had been thinking about purchasing his own dog team to use in the ministry. Because of the difficulty he had experienced on the trip to the Mealy Mountains with Milton, he decided that owning a dog team wasn't for him. Instead, he returned to the States the following year, took flying lessons and purchased an airplane. He planed to use the airplane in Labrador to enhance their church work. After all, flying was faster and less demanding than driving a dog team.

Note: Danny, after training in navigation, ski and pontoon landing and take-off, used his plane in the ministry to a good advantage. He was able to fly over the mountains and lakes with little effort where he had laboriously traveled with Milton and the dog team in previous times. Many times Danny took natives caribou hunting and was able to visit the many small villages scattered along the coast to hold religious services. He used the plane for visiting sick natives who were in the Northwest River Hospital and hauling people from remote areas to and from hospitals where they could receive medical care. Rev. Danny MacKinney went to be with the Lord whom he served on Christmas Eve 1958. He crashed during a storm onto the ice of Goose Bay and was killed instantly. His death wasn't in vain because he touched the lives of a large number of people in Labrador and in the United States.

As a tribute to Danny, a young man who resided in Happy Valley wrote this poem.

DANNY MACKINNEY

He was born in sunny U.S.A.
Where folks just love to dwell,
But he gave up his former birthplace,
His aim was to do God's will.

He flew this lonely coastline
in a single engine plane,
Showing his nerve and stamina
by doing it again and again.

He was always there to help
whenever his need you did claim.
His hopes were to make folks happy
and fly emergencies in his plane.

On Christmas Eve, to cheer the sick children,
to the hospital he did fly.
He gave the children presents,
then happily waved goodbye.

He left Northwest River at three thirty,
to spend Christmas with his friends;
But he plunged to his death at midway.
He would never see home again.

Out there on the ice he lay crumpled
he had finally won life's goal.
When they found him his body was broken,
But not his unconquerable soul

—19—

The Saga Ends

The C-54 lifted off the runway at Goose Bay for the flight to Westover Air Force Base, Massachusetts. There Milton and his wife would take a train to their next duty assignment in Texas.

Below Milton could see the Air Base had changed much since his arrival three years before. There were new buildings in various stages of construction all over the base. When he first came to Goose there were about four hundred men assigned to the Base. Happy Valley had about the same population. Now the Base had expanded to a population of thirty-five hundred service personnel, and Happy Valley's population and grown to over two thousand people. The Air Police squadron had grown to over two hundred men.

He could see row after row of planes from the Strategic Air Command parked in a neat line. There were F-94 Fighter Interceptors parked in another area. It was almost crowded on the flight line.

Once there were only three planes assigned to Goose Bay. He remembered when there were only eighteen men in his police squadron. Things had changed drastically during the past three years. He had spent over two and one-half years living in tents, brush shelters and small cabins during the three years he had spent at Goose Bay.

The plane circled Goose Bay and passed over the western edge of the Mealy Mountains. What had taken minutes by airplane had taken Milton days traveling by dog team. Milton could see the trail of a dog team slowing making its way across Goose Bay toward Northwest River ... a route he had often traveled. Many memories flooded back to him as he peered out the small window of the C-54 recognizing places where he had camped, fished, hunted and traveled by dog team.

He thought about the many people he had arrested or had conflict with while working in the capacity of Base Scout. Some were dismissed from the service. He harbored regrets about a small number of the people he had caused to be punished for infractions of Air Fore regulations.

One incident that he regretted most of all was that of a captain in SAC who was TDY to Goose from Omaha, Nebraska. The Captain was assigned a truck load of Top Secret equipment and was required to have the truck under his direct control at all times. He had to sleep with the truck while TDY.

Milton was patrolling a section of the woodland below the Base when he discovered the truck of classified equipment parked along side a trout stream on a small dirt road. No one was in the immediate area so Milton drove the truck to the nearest guard post and called for a patrol to bring a driver down to take the truck to Air Police Headquarters.

There the truck was turned over to the Commanding Officer of the SAC unit TDY to Goose Bay. The Captain later answered directly to General Curtis Lemay, the Commanding General of the Strategic Air Command. His military career was ruined. All the man had done was assume that the truck would be safe in the woodland while he was nearby fishing.

Milton was saddened to leave Goose Bay. It was like leaving home for the first time. He knew that his new assignment might prove exciting and interesting. He thought of the dog team, the cabin and the natives he had gotten to know so well. Perhaps the future assignment would be a challenge like Goose Bay had been. Only time would tell.

Goodbye, Goose Bay. The Saga had ended.